THE MOTIVATED YOUNG ADULT'S GUIDE TO CAREER SUCCESS AND ADULTHOOD

PROVEN TIPS FOR BECOMING A MATURE ADULT, STARTING A REWARDING CAREER, AND FINDING LIFE BALANCE

BUKKY EKINE-OGUNLANA

TCECPUBLISHING.COM

© Copyright Bukky Ekine-Ogunlana 2021 – All rights reserved.

The content contained within this book may not be reproduced, duplicated or transmitted without direct written permission from the author or the publisher.

Under no circumstance will any blame or legal responsibility be held against the publisher, or author, for any damages, reparation, or monetary loss due to the information contained within this book. Either directly or indirectly. You are responsible for your own choices, actions and results.

Legal Notice:

This book is copyright protected. This book is only for personal use. You cannot amend, distribute, sell, use, quote or paraphrase any part, or the content within this book, without the author or publisher's consent.

Disclaimer Notice:

Please note the information contained within this document is for educational and entertainment purposes only. All effort has been executed to present accurate, up-to-date, and reliable, complete information. No warranties of any kind are declared or implied. Readers acknowledge that the author is not engaging in the rendering of legal, financial, medical or professional advice. The content within this book has been derived from various sources. Please consult a licensed professional before attempting any techniques outlined in this book

By reading this book, the reader agrees that under no circumstances is the author responsible for any losses, direct or indirect, which are incurred as a result of the use of the information contained within this document, including, but not limited to,—errors, omissions, or inaccuracies.

Published by

TCEC Publishing

TCEC House

14-18 Ada Street, London Fields,

E8 4QU, England, Great Britain.

CONTENTS

Introduction — 9

1. Who Is An Adult? — 13
2. When Do You Know You Are An Adult — 23
3. Hidden Truth About Adulthood — 32
4. Adult Learning — 41
5. What Qualifies You As An Adult? — 48
6. Responsibility — 62
7. Career — 81
8. When Should You Begin Your Career? — 94
9. Adult Attitude Adjustment — 101
10. Things You Should Know About Yourself — 109
11. Relationship — 115
12. Balancing Career And Relationship — 128
13. How To Deal With Changes In Life — 142
14. Secrets Of Success For Adults — 155

Conclusion — 169
Other Books You'll Love! — 171
References — 173

DEDICATION

This lovely book is dedicated to all the beautiful students all over the world who, over the years, have passed through the T.C.E.C young adult's program. Thanks for the opportunity to serve you and invest in your colorful and bright future.

Your free gift!

Voucher ID: NGH0001

As a way of saying thank you for purchasing this book, I am offering you a free gift at the end of the book

INTRODUCTION

You may very well be a grown-up, but the odds are you are not. Yes, most of us are walking about in grown-up bodies, but that does not make us adults.

As much as we are excited about being adults, it is not usually as easy as it seems, but many do not know that because we are not adequately educated.

Add to the fact that it is complicated to become an adult. The main reason why this is so tricky is that there are few role models. E.g., look at a list of world leaders and show me one person who is a real adult. Perhaps some of the lesser-known leaders would qualify. If you are a grownup, then you have accomplished something incredible.

However, we cannot help but realize the bitter truth about being an adult, and it is not usually easy to accept.

Our parents did not tell us that we would have to be responsible for ourselves and that the little things we used to ignore would require our effort as adults. We were not told all of that.

We were not told that being an adult would require a high patience level, especially in our careers, and attaining other set goals.

I am sure many of us grew up to realize these things on our own, and we were quite taken aback. The glitz and lure of adulthood is not such a fantastic ride.

We could go on and on with it, but then that is not the point. This book is here to provide answers to these questions as well as every other thing that is required to being a responsible and successful adult in life.

The truth is that not everyone would be the ideal adult because everyone is different. However, getting this book is taking a step towards becoming the perfect adult everyone expects you to be.

One thing to be noted is that getting this book is not just the end. After all, it is not a magical book that just transforms you from mere reading. Therefore, reading to understand is very important.

Once you understand and practice what you have read here, you are way ahead of others and on the journey to being a well-adjusted adult capable of handling with ease whatever it is that life throws at you.

I do not want to spend a lot of time convincing you to get this book, but if you do get it, you are on the right path to being that adult you have always envisaged yourself to be.

We are about to embark on a life-changing experience with this book, and I am excited as you are. I wish you good luck.

Let us get started!

After reading this book, please feel free to leave a review based on your findings and how useful the book was to you. I would be incredibly thankful if you could take 60 seconds to write a brief review on the platform of purchase, even if it's just a few sentences!

WHO IS AN ADULT?

Suppose I say an adult is a person who is 18 years or older unless the matter is drinking legally, in which case an adult is someone 21 years or older. That is a start. But we are not so much interested in legal definitions as changing conceptions of who an adult is. You could argue that unless we know who an adult is, we do not know who a person is or who a human being is.

Aristotle said that to know what the thing is, one needed to know its final cause. For example, I could display to you a corkscrew, a piece of wood with a spiraling wire descending from it. I would explain that it is for removing corks from wine bottles. That is what it was invented and created for. That, for Aristotle, was its final cause.

The Final Cause of a living organism is the function that the organism performs typically when it reaches maturity. The form or structure it develops and evolves through childhood should help it accomplish these functions well when it reaches maturity. To understand and get what humans are, we need to know what we expect fully grown adult humans to be.

> *A couple had a beautiful bouncing baby girl called Amy. She was so young and fragile that she had to depend on her parents for everything, especially her mother. From accommodation to feeding and all other provisions, Amy solely relied on her parents.*
> *They decided what she wore, the school she went to, and even the type of friends she made.*
> *It is very safe to say that Amy is still a*
> ***CHILD.***

An adult is a person who takes 100 % responsibility for his or her life and situation. That is, nothing is someone else's fault. The words "It's not fair" do not occur to you. An adult or grownup takes responsibility for his or her emotions. In other words, no one else makes you feel the way you do. An adult is honest with himself or herself. That is, no self-deception, no pretending. You see people and situations as they are and find a way to respond to them.

*Amy has grown to a particular age, and she does not want to be associated with the term 'child' anymore. After all, she is 18 and is legally an adult. Therefore, she can decide what she wants to do with her life. She has gotten to an age where she can make some significant decisions without her parents' and even friends' influence. However, is this what it takes to be an **ADULT**?*

You do not just become a grown-up when you turn eighteen. Adulting is a process. It takes many trial and error and stern reminders or hints from life and expired relationships. Although we sprout, grow up and acquire tools, responsibilities, and trades, deep inside, we are still children who snap back often. Whenever or at any time we encounter resistance or triggers, our child rears its reactive head. We pout, whine, and complain. Adulting is a practice. It takes years and years to become aware of our child and stop pulling from whom we used to be once or how we were handled and treated.

Adulthood is not centered on a particular age but one's ability to work and handle whatever life throws at him or her. Your ability to handle situations, whether emotionally, mentally, and even psychologically, are essential factors that will determine how much of an adult you are. If your reactions to situations are always emotional or irrational, it does not matter if you are 70 years old. You would still be a child mentally.

Not long ago, Mrs. Harrison realized that she had not entirely made the transition to adulthood. She had attained an adequate level of emotional intelligence. She was keenly aware of her emotions and controlled them very well. Where she fell short was her lack of sensitivity to other's feelings. She thought she was sensitive and even prided herself on her ability to "see" others. She thought of herself as a mature adult, after all.

In her work, she often advised people on what to do and how to do it. She often facilitated processes for various groups. She wrote and published three books. She gave lectures on personal responsibility, leadership, and spirituality. Yet, she came to realize that she was not a 58-year-old adult. She was more like a 15-year-old with 43 years of experience. Most 15-year-olds are at the center of their universe. "Everything revolves around them." Although she practiced unselfishness and often cared about others, her perspective was a center of attention.

As a center of attention, she expected people and situations to cater to her. She was often frustrated with other people. When someone told her something personal, she related it to herself rather than truly understanding them. As children, we are all centers of attention. We expect the "adults" in our respective lives to provide for us to give us what we need. She did not expect people to give her food or money, but she did expect people to meet her emotional needs.

And she had it on the authority of her "grown-up" son that she had not been an adult either. He is 35 years old and becoming an adult. He has never met a good role model--not his parents, none of his teachers at secondary/high school or university, no managers in the workplace, and his field, which is Art, no artists that he has met. He had to figure it out on his own.

"Me too," said Mrs. Harrison.

Although her son certainly has catalyzed her.

Perhaps the most significant realization has been that her ego is like that of a child. All egos are children. Anyone who is run by their ego cannot function as an adult. The ego is the center of attention. An adult is a center of influence. That is, as a center of influence, you realize that your thoughts and emotions have a ripple effect. This ripple effect has a lot of influence as well as an impact on people around you.

Everything that you think, feel, say, and do affects the people and the situations around you. This is a change in perspective from *"How is everyone and everything affecting me?"* to *"how are everyone and everything affected by me?"* It is an understanding that life is not happening to me. I am creating it with my every thought, with my deeply embedded assumptions, values, and beliefs. The meaning we perceive in people and things are the meaning we have assigned to them.

An adult questions assumptions--his or her own and everyone else's beliefs too. In other words, as an adult, you think rather than parrot the thoughts of others. It is difficult to subscribe to people's preferences if you are an adult. If you do subscribe, you probably do not subscribe to all of it. Everything that shows up in both your thoughts and in your life gets questioned: "Is it true?" If you are truthful, you will find that most of them are not. You will find that most of everything people hold to be true is being made up apart from the Bible, which contains THE TRUTH.

As you enter adulthood, it will seem to be a struggle at first. You are releasing cherished beliefs. You are letting go of your need for approval, for control over others, and your habit of accepting "truths" that just are not true. For example: "You can have whatever you want!" Many have spoken that "truth," but it is not valid. You cannot have whatever you want. Therefore, so many of us got frustrated after trying so many books and programs without success.

You can have what you TRULY want. You can only if you know what you want, so ask yourself the following questions, *what do you truly want? What is important to you?* Do not answer that question too quickly. These are not questions that you just answer sparingly because you feel you have the answers readily available. Set aside your fiction and your goals. Get quick, and ask the question. What do I want? Listen within. Keep asking if need be, given that we most identify with our egos, an excellent way to inquire may be: "Not my will, but thy will be done."

Once your answers begin to flow, act on them. That is the other trait of an adult; the ability to move forward courageously, to do what you are instructed to do from inside. Perhaps the most important thing that we could say qualifies us as an adult, the ability to listen to our inner man and do something based on internal instincts and not due to some external factor/influence.

So, are you an adult or not? Be honest. If you are, you already know it. This book does not evoke any emotion for you. Reading this book does not automatically make you an adult, nor does it qualify you as a responsible one. You alone know the things you feel as you read this book.

So, deep down, if you know you are not, then maybe it is time to start growing up. It is worth the effort. The reward is freedom and the power of 100 % responsibility. The bonus is the joy you get knowing that you cannot be anyone's victim. You will find out that you need not participate in any more dramas or soap operas in life. And as you release your fears, worries, resentments, and disappointments, that there is a stronger voice within you that will guide you.

Instead of hoping certain things will happen for you (as children do), you trust that your conscience, which is the door to your spirit, will guide you well. You will form intentions from what you have fed your heart with, and those intentions will bubble up from within you. You will sense knowing that the path you intend is the right one. You will accept, but not judge, that most others are still children and do your best to be helpful--to be the role model we so desperately need.

Thus, life is all about understanding what to do, where to do what, and when what you need to do will occur. Adulthood may be a difficult phase, but it is not a license for you to blame and criticize others when things do not go your way.

Being an adult is much more than just dressing smart and earning money from work. Adulthood comes with many responsibilities and sacrifices to be made along the line so before you call yourself an ***adult***, ask yourself if you are ready to go through all of these.

If you feel you are, you must ascertain and judge if you are mentally and emotionally prepared because being an adult is not just limited to the things we think we know, so you have to bear all of these in mind.

I am sure that you have a more enlightened grasp and understanding of who an adult is from all you have read in this chapter. Having a vision of this concept in mind will help you navigate the adulthood phase quicker.

WHEN DO YOU KNOW YOU ARE AN ADULT

The age when you become an adult is open to interpretation in many households. There are those 12-year old's who think they are 17 and then 35-year old's who prefer to stay at home, being looked after and avoiding the personal and financial responsibilities of being independent.

In most countries, adulthood can be said to have been attained between the ages of 16 to 18, with 18 being the generally accepted legal age for being an adult.

Astrologically, the late '20s are deemed to be the age when young people enter adulthood. This often equates to when they start settling into making responsible lifestyle choices, committing to a career, home, relationship, and perhaps even starting a family.

This time can be delayed by years spent at university, taking a gap year, the impact of student debt, establishing a career or business, saving the deposit to buy a first home - any of these can defer leaving home and becoming independent.

However, this appears not to be so for many people out there, which poses the question, ***so when do you know you are an adult?***

I asked some teens to tell me what they think being an adult is and how they will know adults. Here is what they said:

Angelica C

> *I will know that I am an adult when I can live on my own when I am fully capable of surviving independently. I will no longer depend on shelter, food, transportation, and money from my parents. I feel that an adult does not mean that you just turn eighteen. For me, being an adult means someone older than eighteen who is capable of living without expenses from one's parents. I think that many*

people, especially teenagers, think being an adult means turning eighteen because you are "free." However, just like Uncle Ben from Spiderman says, "With great power comes great responsibility." As one gets older, one obtains more responsibility. When a teenager turns eighteen, they have a lot of responsibility: paying for their car, home, school, food, and other necessities. To me, if a teenager can take those responsibilities, then they are considered an adult. I honestly believe that many Hispanic teenagers who are eighteen or older are not adults because most of them, at least in my neighborhood, still depend on their parents. I plan on being an adult when I turn eighteen and graduate high school. Hopefully, I can receive scholarships to pay for my college education and dorm costs. If that works, I will consider myself an adult because my parents will not pay for anything.

Maria V

I will know that I am an adult when I find my passion in life. What I mean by "passion in life" is what you want to do in life. For exam-

ple, when you are little, you want to be a fireman, policeman, doctor, teacher, etc.... As you get much older, you start to see what you are interested in. Once you hit secondary/high school and have a career that calls for your attention, then I think you are mature because you have a future ahead of you, you are thinking of college, and you know that you are making the right decision.

Andrea G

I have no slightest idea how I will know I am an adult. I asked my friends around me when they all thought they would feel like a grown-up, and they all said, "I don't think you can ever stop growing," "You may get old, but you never stop growing spiritually, emotionally, and mentally." For me, I found that to be very inspirational. When you think about it...It is true, there is no point in your life that someone says you are an adult. I believe that it is just a way to label people and target a specific age group.

I will consider myself an adult when I feel old enough, have kids, am married, and have a job that I love. I think this way because there is no evidence that you are an adult when you turn a certain age. I think people say that you are an adult when your brain fully matures, and it has reached its peak, but boys and girls grow at different rates, and you cannot assume all girls and all boys. Another thing is that everyone has a distinct personality, biochemistry, and hormones.

There can be times of mixed emotions when we are faced with adulthood. When we are faced with reality, we need to be serious and provide a voice of authority or reason. Our children may have said or done something wrong, naughty or dangerous, and as much as we would love to laugh along with them, we really ought to act as responsible adults and chastise them for their behavior.

Neither do we want to pass on unfortunate habit patterns to our children, like an extreme over-reaction to spiders or cockroaches, or have them witness negative traits and characteristics that we might have imbibed from when we were young too. Being a good role model is essential when we are adults because everything we do is reflected in others' attitudes and behavior.

Or maybe that our parents are becoming increasingly frail and reliant on us, so that we must be the responsible adult who determines what happens to support their care, maybe by taking out a power of attorney or signing a DNR (a do not resuscitate order) in case they become infirmed or when they are gravely ill. Parenting our parents pushes us into serious adult mode.

What about our relationships? Often, they evolve with each person acquiring their regular tasks. One may tend the garden, balance their finances, and look after the car while the other attends more domestic chores. But what happens if one person goes on strike or, for some reason, fails to undertake their agreed duties. Sometimes, when things do not go our way, we may see our inner person emerging by way of sulking, temper tantrums, retaliation, and tears - hardly an adult response!

Now, this is by no means invalidating your emotional response to things. Of course, it's fair to get angry sometimes. You are allowed to cry sometimes when things are not going your way, whatever it is, you are only human to feel that way, but what qualifies you as an adult is how well you manage these emotions, especially how you show these emotions to others.

There are ways that you can use to handle such situations without losing control. You must understand that there are approaches to these things, and you must navigate these feelings. Discussing how we feel about what has happened or gone wrong and then negotiating a way forward can be a better response. Maybe it is a good time to redefine our roles, delegate several tasks, or buy additional help, bringing communications back onto a more adult footing.

And do not forget the childlike joy in life that we may never want to lose, the excitement at visiting a funfair, hearing an ice cream van, seeing the first snowfall of the year, running along a beach. Nurturing our sense of innocence and treasuring it adds another dimension to being an adult. That sense of fun, elation, the joy of being alive is an exceptional part of finding balance in being an adult.

> *For Jonathan, it was hard settling into adulthood. For him, it was not about starting up a career, family, or even buying a property. It started when he had to go to college at 17.*

Coming from a family where things were not so good, it was upon him to cater to some needs without waiting for his parents' input. He had to shuffle between school and work over at some drugstore close to the campus over at college. At 17, he had learned some hard lessons and gone through some experiences that even some adults would never have dreamt of ever experiencing. It did not matter that he was young and all. Life had dealt with him with some hefty blows.

Therefore, you need to understand that your age does not necessarily determine if you are an adult or not, so you must be able to decipher whether you want to identify with the term 'adult' as you attain a certain age.

As much as the thought of being addressed as an adult can be quite thrilling, it can also be slightly frightening for some people. At such times, they are not sure they should be referred to as an adult just yet.

When do you know you are an adult? There are a lot of disagreement on the right time to associate with the term adulthood. From what we have read so far in this book, one thing is for sure: maturity is subjective and has different meanings and explanations to other individuals.

There is no definite time stated for an adult, and they're probably will never be. However, emotional, mental, social, psychological, and financial growth can be the criteria in which one can assume the role of being an adult.

HIDDEN TRUTH ABOUT ADULTHOOD

There was a time in our lives where we looked at the adults back then and wished that we were all grown-up. In essence, we all wanted to be ADULTS so badly that we would even go as far as playing dress-up and imitating the adults in our lives.

However, as we start to attain puberty and move through the teenage phase, we begin to realize that things are not as they appear to be, and it begins to feel like the whole idea of adulthood was a sham

As we grow up and assume the much-anticipated role of being an adult, we start to realize that there are some harsh truths that our parents did not talk to us about.

As this reality starts to hit you in the face, you will understand why some adults always seem to be unhappy with themselves and others around them. They are not bitter people; they find it more challenging to cope with adulthood's harsh realities.

It is essential for you as a young adult to understand and know some of these hidden truths about the world of adulthood as knowing these will better equip you with adequately coping with these hidden and often hard truths about adults' world.

First, **you will realize that you start to lose touch with everyone and everything.** Do not get this wrong. You are not sinking into depression or coming down with a mental illness. It is just one of the bitter truths about adulthood.

> *As I began to step into the threshold of being an adult, I started to feel very differently about some things. At first, I thought I was depressed because I did not understand why I did not react to something with as much enthusiasm as I used to when I was relatively young.*

It was or is probably the same for you. Things and people that used to interest you and make you happy do not appeal to you anymore, and you are not easily excited about hangouts, holidays, and even gifts.

You will notice that you do not talk to people as much as you used to. Some friends would fade to the background as everyone would become busy working and living their lives. While it can be a painful experience, it is usually bound to happen.

Trust me. You are not losing yourself. You are going through a phase that no one prepared you for. These are some of the things that you probably never knew would happen as you grew older. You do not have to be friends with people you grew up with.

As a famous African proverb says,

> "Twenty friends cannot be friends for twenty years."

Therefore, it is essential to know that these things would happen. People drift apart and lose the connection you once had. However, you must note this and learn how to handle this so that you do not end up pushing people away and severing significant ties with those that matter.

Another hidden truth about adulthood is that **although maturity comes with freedom, you will not always be free**. We are all excited and happy at the prospect of being adults and being open to doing whatever we want without interference. You will, over time, come to realize that it is not what it seems. As much as you have attained freedom as an adult, you will discover that you are not free to do what you want.

"Immediately, I got off of college and started to work. I quickly realized and visualized that things were not going to be as I envisaged them to be. I had always thought that being an adult meant I had more freedom to do whatever I wanted, have fun, and stay out if I wanted. I was soon caught up with work that I barely had time for something as easy as grocery shopping, talk more of even going out, or hanging out with friends.

Whatever free time I had was spent sleeping in bed and trying to prepare myself for the next week of work. It was like I was free to do the things I wanted but still did not hold onto

> *my freedom. Nobody ever told me it was going to be like this "*

— DAVID OWEN

You might have the finances to go all out, but there is no time to have fun because, as an adult, the fun would be the last thing on your mind as working and daily living would take away your time mostly.

As a young adult, you will also realize that **you are responsible for yourself and accountable to others**. As you start to live the life of an adult, you will realize that those little things you used to take for granted do take a tremendous effort.

> *For example, you always used to go to your parents for money to get stuff, and when you did not get your demands met, you would throw tantrums and think they purposely do not want to help you out.*
>
> *As a grown-up, you will start to see things from their perspective and understand the reasons for their actions. As you start earning,*

you will realize that extravagant spending is not ideal.

One other thing is that you will realize that people now look up to you, and you owe them explanations for every rational and irrational decision you make, especially your family members.

Therefore, you must be responsible for your dealings and take actions that will prove you can handle adulthood and increase the confidence others have in you.

Another hidden truth about being an adult is that **you start to say NO more often**. As a child and growing teenager, it was always easy to agree to things people around us want, like choosing to go to the mall because your friends want you to even when you know that you have assignments to work on.

We all had moments like this where we prioritize what our friends wanted because we could not say NO. Well, adulthood changes all of that. You learn to say "no" a lot, especially to close friends and family members.

I remember the first time with my friend. Jenny

and I had been friends from 3rd grade. We were very close and did almost everything together. The thing about Jenny was that she always made the major decisions. She decided on the places we went, the people we chose as friends, and all of that. All through high school and even down to college, it was always like that, mostly as we both attended the same university. There were times when I was not cool with some of the things she suggested, but she had a way of making me do the things she wanted regardless. It got to a certain point where I had to tell myself that I could not always do what she wanted. As expected, she was livid and could not comprehend why I was refusing to hang out with her and do the things we used to do together. I tried to let her know that something had to change because we have both grown and had to live our lives as different individuals now with responsibilities to handle. Things went sour between us, and the friendship was not as strong as it used to be, but I did not regret telling her NO because I knew it was the right thing to do at that point.

Now, this may make you feel self-centered and appear too mean, but that is just one of the things that come with being an adult that you never knew would happen. As an adult, you will understand that learning to say NO sometimes is suitable for your emotional, physical, and mental wellbeing.

Finally, one more truth about adulthood is that **we realize that we become more selfish with our time.** This may look weird because while growing up, we have always been taught that being selfish is bad. While this is true in some sense, you realize that it is necessary to be selfish as an adult.

By selfish, I mean you start to cherish the little time you get to yourself. Rather than jump at every opportunity to go to an outing, event, mall, etc., you start to realize that you would rather chill at home, cuddled up in bed with a blanket and popcorn, and just watch your favorite movie.

> *Jessy recently opened up about not having a social life at all, especially since she clocked 26. When she was asked why she said she recently started feeling old as little things no longer interest her. She has begun to prefer binge-watching movies to hanging out with*

her friends. She said she had begun to feel too old lately. She wished she could go back to being a child.

It is funny but real, and I am sure that as adults, we all feel these things, and even as young adults, you may have started to experience these feelings in small doses. You cannot always give to others without giving to yourself. Therefore, it is okay to put yourself first before others.

You must understand that these experiences would not be the same for everyone, and the list is never-ending, but for the sake of the book, we will discuss just five of them.

However, every adult would have experienced these things at some point. If you have not, do not feel like something is wrong with you. You must understand that these are just processes of adult life.

All of these are some concealed truths about being an adult that we never knew about. While being an adult can be fun, it will not always be fun but what is important is learning to deal with these truths and knowing that it is all part of being an adult.

ADULT LEARNING

Have you ever thought of asking yourself a question about your adulthood? Have you ever wondered why your adulthood is not as pleasant as studying new skills in your childhood? Do you know you can become a child while learning and an adult while knowing and acting?

One thing should be clear to us: Education is a life-long process from birth till death. There is no specific period when education is going to stop. From the day a child is born till their last breath, they need education for a spectacular memory that will be kept for posterity. Every day we learn new things, and there is never a time where we stop acquiring knowledge. This can be in the form of personal experiences, stories you must have learned from others, and so much more. These serve to educate us, so learning is bound to take place as long as one lives.

An individual who refuses to give herself or himself to proper tutoring has surrendered him/herself to mediocrity. There is nothing as hurtful as watching your contemporaries exploit while you remain stagnant with the baseless excuse that you are old. An enlightened mind is a compelling one, and you are equipped with the power to do things that others did not deem possible. After all, knowledge is power.

Have you ever thought of the logic and reasons why education is almost a compulsory part of everyone's lives? From the time you were born, you were taught to speak, feel, and learn new things even as a child. You were enrolled in school to learn more and become educated. Everything served as a lesson because learning is one of the keys to surviving in our world.

Many people achieve most of their feats in their adulthood stage. It is not that they never wanted to accomplish those things at their prime, but circumstances beyond them pushed it further. Their resilient spirit kept pushing them till they could achieve that which they have dreamed of becoming.

This is not an advocate that you need to wait till you are closer to the grave before you start to achieve. It is just to let you know that there is no stipulated time that learning can stop. It is infinite. Before your birth, people were learning; after your delivery, people learn; after your death, people will learn.

You must understand that part of being a productive individual and being a citizen of any country is to learn a way to give to society and not be a burden to society. In this vein, governments are tasked to provide free education to their citizens, and in turn, all citizens have the responsibility to acquire education for their benefit. It should never be a take-take situation. It should be a give-and-take situation where you have something to offer to the government asides from seeking things you can get from them.

It is also applicable in the way you relate to people around you. Always learn new ways to help those around you and not always seek the things you can get from others. For example, in typical African societies, the children are usually trained to go to school to help the family.

Indeed, children go to school to learn how to read, write, and do math, and they continue to amass new knowledge and skills as they grow older. And after graduating from university, and now as adults, they are expected to get a job or try their hands at putting up their own business and become responsible adults and citizens. But learning is not supposed to stop after graduation; it should continue long after finishing academic pursuits in school.

Bryan D

After I got out of university, I thought that was the end of reading books and staying up all night reading. I had thought that I would not have to bother with anything that had to do with racking my brain mentally. That was not the case because even at work, I learn new things every day, and these things require me to research and know more about them. I understand every day, even when I do not feel up to it. One thing I have learned is that education is not restricted to the four walls of a classroom.

Adult learning should be one of our priorities as education should be a lifelong process, never stopping at one body of knowledge but going through different disciplines to make a person well-rounded and knowledgeable. Of course, this is quite impossible in the real world - no one can know everything there is to know. However, you could always have a reason to want to learn more. That is to have self-improvement and become qualified for more responsibilities, especially at work, to aim for a promotion or a salary increase. It is vital to know everything about a particular subject and, at least, a little of everything.

Adult learning is quite different from what we have gone through as children and during our teens. Young people would lack self-direction and autonomy that allow learning to proceed unimpeded. Adults can direct themselves towards their real goal in life, acquire the basics of life experiences, and possess practical knowledge about family relationships and work responsibilities through their previous formal school education. Adults want to learn something that can lead to realizing their goals, and they would be willing to go through any training if they are relevant to what they are after. Because they are practical, they can focus on lessons proven to be useful in their work line.

We can find many adults today who are willing to learn new skills but are hesitant to take the first steps. They think that there are no more opportunities to acquire new knowledge and much less to live by what they would have learned because they have passed their prime. They are afraid that they will not find any open doors that would lead them to a renewed career path. But this is just not true. You can find plenty of help when it comes to adult learning opportunities. You can find many online offers for career advice that is right for you. You can contact them over the phone or through email and ask for career advice.

We have recently heard stories about older people going back to college and getting their degrees. It goes to show how much schooling and education are essential. There is no limit to what you can obtain and the knowledge you can acquire once you put your mind to it. There are several ways you can make out what you want to achieve.

You can go through self-assessment by asking yourself what exactly is it that you want to achieve at this point in your life. Can you afford to learn new skills and knowledge, or can you afford not to? One relevant question that you should not forget to ask is the timing - is this the right time to take adult education classes? On a personal level, are you disciplined enough to go through the lessons?

Many adult learning courses are designed to take advantage of today's technology, which usually means through online classes that you could access anywhere in the world where you could bring a computer. There is an internet connection. You do not have to sit inside a physical classroom if that is what you are afraid of. Some are designed to let you learn through volunteer work in your community or by researching your local library.

With new technologies and social services such as Google Classroom, HubSpot, Udemy, and other online learning platforms, people, especially adults of any age, can sit from the comfort of their homes and acquire an education that is made readily available to them and receive a certification after that.

WHAT QUALIFIES YOU AS AN ADULT?

How many adults do you know? Who exactly is an adult? My severe and light-hearted response when asked about adults? - *"Don't let the big bodies twit you!"* Adults are neither as universal as you might naively guess nor as rare as you might reasonably expect. That does not imply that there are all that many out there, and what do I mean? If you look up the word "mature" in the same dictionary, you will find "fully developed, as a person, a mind, etc." It seems somewhat circular. Does anyone know what is being described? What are we even talking about?

It is also easy to come across a slew of quotes that ennoble children and ridicule adults. Are all these just so-called that grownups are envious of and yearning for the joyful, carefree, playfulness of youth and employing self-deprecatory humor that is cheaply aimed at adults' mundane responsibilities and muted effect?

Just look at what adults do. Adults usually engage in gainful employment regularly; take care of their self-, wife/husband, family, and extended family care. Adults are answerable for their life commitments, including job, bill paying, house chores, upkeep, and being as good as their word. Adults are held liable for what they sign up to do in their public community / private lives, such as writing, writing, doing, and saying.

Grownups are held accountable for their actions and commitments in life, whether that is in a relationship, marriage, or friendship, in a work environment with meeting both the letter and spirit of their job details and description, and in the community being a worthwhile citizen regarding keeping their house and courtyard kept up, being informed of community issues and well-being in addition to political candidates and public issues, and regularly engaging in the voting proceedings. When you watch what grownups do, this does have a ring of maturity in being fully developed as a person. Being an adult in all these forms is rather a high watermark to meet for almost all of us.

So, you might ask, what is so hard in being an adult after all? Well, to state the pronounced, it isn't one bit easy, and hardly will it be getting more comfortable with all the modern times in which the Western world brings in terms of diversions, entertainments, distractions, mobile devices, gaming platforms/games, internet, speed of life, governmental regulation, dealing with bureaucracies and the exponentially increasing stuff of life to somehow fit into the same twenty- four hours a day, one hundred and sixty-eight hours a week, just like anyone else.

Who has the passionate desirous fire in the tummy? Who has space or time? Is it all to race faster away from all the ego-mind's saber-rattling worries, ultimately of after-life, annihilation, nothingness, or running more quickly toward all the ego-minds dream up is selfish gratifications, greedy attachments, and wants of media-manipulation into supposed needs? It is like being captured in a vice, somewhere amid rock and a hard spot, all orchestrated and choreographed courtesy of one imaginary, abstract, ego-mind or self.

It is proposed that self-responsibility or self-accountability is the quintessential defining attribute to qualify as an adult. The word responsibility means "response-ability," that is, possessing the ability to respond. Self-responsibility means not only deciding, choosing but further participating in an engaged, responsive, most efficient possible fashion or form in taking responsibility or liability for your entire full life. See the attribute of being responsible for one's individuality as having the capacity, the willingness, and enacting in the behavior (sometimes called "praxis") of a continuing moment to moment.

Self-responsibility can be displayed and seen in taking care of doing and actioning what you said, promised, plighted, and signed up to do, without any if's, but's, blaming others, rationalizations, reasons, or sniveling excuses for not doing what there is to be done if there is some way within the parameters of reality to do it honorably.

This character feature of self-responsibility is synonymous with self-accountability. In a like fashion, accountability means "account-ability," that is, owning the ability and capacity to account for your own life. To be self-accountable means to be amenable to the obligations and duties you have in your life by the very nature of being alive as a human being in the web of life on planet Earth. Anyone who is self-accountable answers fundamentally to him- or herself in honoring a code of living, ethics, and honesty that goes to the depth of who every one of us is, on the highest, broadest, and most profound of levels, and ultimately on the indwelling and transcendent Divine realm. It is simple and not easy to ever approach comprehensively to inhabit this vision as much as we can.

While this view is the top of the top, what are the critical building blocks that create a solid foundation for enabling and empowering anyone to inhabit self-accountability or self-responsibility? Consider some keys to get in gear and count on God's word to you and yourself as your authority in life:

Presence

That is, the practice of living in the present moment: Only by turning up in this here-and-now bit can self-responsibility and self-accountability come on-line and be legitimate. Also, add the respectful skill of witnessing, that is, in presence standing aside to observe who we think we are (the imaginary or fake sense of self or ego) to reveal, see-through, and dissolve its fake authority and fear-driven influence.

Honesty

That is, sticking the straight-up, nothing left out, truth in life: Purely by playing with a full-deck in being a stand-up guy or person can anyone take responsibility and accountability for his or her own life.

Stalwart

That is, exhibiting reliable, stable, and disciplined words and actions: When anyone has honest traversed an extended learning curve, much like schooling in the trenches of long, challenging, and smart job and often as a pupil with one or more mentors, any abilities truly built and owned communicates a reliable, stable, disciplined and an aware sense of oneself in having some clear idea what makes you tick.

Congruent

That is, words, actions, body language, facial expression, and tone of voice all communicate the same message of clarity: When one's being and the whole body sends an undivided message and a singular across all levels of expression, what gets transmitted is something more significant than the sum of these parts-it communicates trust and confidence that what is seen, heard, and experienced is more real, authentic, and accurate.

Not knowing and being open

To bring the maturity to full value, not knowing and staying wide open and prone to changes, translates into being available to all inputs, creativity, possibilities, brainstorming, innovation, and perspectives in every stratum of life you might find yourself, all of which are core attributes to yielding and developing self-responsibility and self-accountability.

Win-Win/Non-Zero-Sum Game

Being a mature adult entails shedding the me-me-me primitive ego's connection to itself and performing a much bigger game of what works for everyone, merely a win-win or non-zero-sum game. Here one brings a perspective of no scarcity of anything and a surplus of everything for everyone to meet life's demands.

A rock-solid responsibility in operation to grow

Possibly the rarest character feature and trait on the planet is for human beings to bring-a rock-solid commitment in action to grow. To bring the publicly stated intention to grow, a time and place for this to occur, and indirect activities' follow-through to completion. The three components of a commitment are to be accomplished regularly. It points to a committed person with self-responsibility and self-accountability that are palpably self-evident.

There is no stopping of such a being in any set of circumstances in powerfully harnessing and channeling their energies, talents, skills, and abilities in transforming and transcending all obstacles and inhabiting their full creative expression. This may well be the most significant character trait and personality attribute you can bring to any transformational process, whether expressed in a therapeutic process, meeting the highly challenged circumstances relationships regularly present or ineffectively facing, and dealing with change in its multitude of disguises. However, it arises in this present moment.

Apart from that, other things qualify you as an adult. One more thing that allows you as an adult is to craft an identity for yourself is making independent decisions for yourself, especially without external influence.

At this point, you must make conscious decisions on the commitments you need to make, the relationships you want to be in, and the career you would like to take, etc. Making these decisions without influence or control from other people qualifies you as an adult.

While it seems cool to talk about all these things that qualify you as an adult, we must admit that one of the most important traits or factors that can prepare you as an adult is **FINANCIAL INDEPENDENCE.**

You may be so excited to be an adult, but you cannot be an adult without having enough resources to take care of your immediate and future needs. Therefore, young adults need to thrive for financial independence, especially as they are just emerging into the world of adulthood, so that things, especially expenses, would be easier to handle.

You cannot be wholly referred to as an adult if you still depend on your family to take care of your expenses. The reason why every adult is involved in one business or career is basically to source for finances. There is no other feeling that is as liberating as knowing that you do not depend on anybody to fend for yourself.

Financial independence may be essential, but one thing that should not be ignored is that one needs to be patient in all of these. **Patience** is a necessary virtue that emerging adults need to learn. While we all want to do the things that qualify us as full and capable adults, one thing should be understood: things will not always go as planned.

You won't start as the best or most responsible adult out there. You will not be automatically rich and be independent financially overnight. It will take months, and even up to ten years, you will make mistakes. Sometimes you would feel the need to give up, but learn to be patient with yourself in all of these.

As mundane as it sounds, patience is perhaps one of the most outstanding qualities one must possess to qualify as an adult. Learn to be patient with yourself as every day is a day to learn and unlearn things. You are not superhuman, and things will not go your way with the snap of a finger, so you must trust the process and be patient. Peer pressure might be a huge factor as you start to think you are not doing enough compared to others' achievements. Therefore, it is essential to be patient with yourself and the growth process. Therefore, learning to be patient with yourself qualifies you as an adult.

Signs that You have Matured in life

People say that with age comes maturity. However, this is not always the case. Sometimes, those who are younger are even more mature than people who are older than them. Maturity is not weighted or measured by age but by one's understanding and experience in life.

Take a closer look at the clues or signs that shows you that you have become more "mature" than you were before.

- **You are valuing your time.** You will realize that your time is your most valuable resource. Hence, you will make sure that every second is being spent wisely. You avoid sleeping in on the weekends and dedicate your precious time to doing productive things that can help you advance in your profession, grow, and mature in life.

- **You make sure that everything is planned out carefully**. As much as possible, you avoid making impulse decisions. Be it buying a new bag, attending events, and even running your errands, you make sure that everything is planned up to the dot.
- **You prioritize your health and wellbeing**. You no longer care or worry about what other people say about you if you and the people you care about know the truth. You value your wellbeing and inner peace more than the opinion of those people around you.
- **You prefer staying in than going out**. Your perfect Friday night would be to stay at home in your pajamas while watching your favorite shows and eating a box of pizza (either by yourself or with a loved one). A Friday night out in loud places no longer interests you. You simply want peace and the simple joys of enjoying having time to yourself. - If you feel like those points mentioned above, do not apply to you and are still not "adult enough"? What should you do?
- **Transform your mindset**. If anyone tells you that you are not adult enough, it may be because of the way you think and react to

certain things. Therefore, you must transform and change your mindset. Train yourself not to respond to everything that is happening around you. Train yourself not to listen to and spread any form of "gossip." Not everything needs your reaction.

- **Always be mindful of your actions**. Be aware of the things you are doing and how it is affecting others. Remember that the world does not revolve around you, and you must be considerate of the people around you.
- **Learn to take responsibility**. If you made a mistake, admit it. Do not justify your actions even though you know that what you did is wrong, and you have hurt other people's feelings. Take responsibility for your actions and whatever damage it has caused. Ask for forgiveness without justifying what you have done, and make up for your mistakes.
- **Surround yourself with the right people**. You become the average of the five people you spend most of your time with, so make sure you are in the right group. Avoid engaging with too loud people who confidently do "illicit" things and display a reckless attitude and behavior. If you want to

be more mature, surround yourself with the people who are focused on doing things that will contribute to their growth, those who have ethical principles and values, and those who would not lead you astray.

RESPONSIBILITY

Being an adult means that you have a specific role to be fulfilling. It is usually associated with finding your purpose for living, which is generally expressed in daily activities or jobs. Unless you are self-employed/employed in a position that matches the ideal career you hope to attain, you are likely willing to file away and possibly forget about the dreams you once had - because society expects that an adult is supposed to be responsible. While you may start with a specific plan based upon a vision you believe God has shown to you, your interests, or your academic achievements, you may have settled for something else because of need or out of necessity.

The reasons for settling for a job that is not within your dreams' parameters may include financial obligations, limited job choices, a competitive job market, or any other number of reasons that leave you with a perception that there are limited options. And once you have settled on and accepted a position, you may likely stay in that job for many of those same reasons. But it is possible that you can have an adequate job, one that pays the bills, and still sustain your dreams of the future because that will serve as a motivating source for change.

What Society Expects

Children are naturally imaginative and usually good with pretending until they are taught about life's realities. They can dream and develop ideas that have no limitations. Their ability to act out scenarios and pretend is not defined by anything other than what they are interested in at that moment. And it may be easy to dismiss their fun because they are "just kids." Children are required to attend mandatory education where they are taught to be dependent upon their teacher, and they learn the skills needed to become productive citizens.

As children become young adults, they have an idea of what it means to be responsible, and they may begin to formulate plans for work after graduation from secondary/high school. Once they have graduated, society considers them to be adults, and then they are now expected to be responsible. They may already be working or just starting in their career - and over time, their dreams can be forgotten in the pursuit of a reliable and steady job, which means they are doing what is expected of them.

Tobi A

When I had graduated from college, I did not know what to do with my life, to be honest. I had studied Mechanical Engineering, but I did not feel like I could find any befitting job in my country. It was hard enough finding a mediocre job, but a career as a mechanical engineer was much harder. That, however, wasn't the scariest part of it all. What was scary was how much my parents and extended family members expected the best from me, and it was hard, knowing I could disappoint them and act beneath their expectations.

Developing a Career Path

A career's start requires focused attention as skills are being learned and productive habits are being developed. Suppose the job was as a result of careful planning and the completion of academic goals. In that case, there will likely be a feeling of satisfaction because a specific plan has been worked through - and it may feel like the ideal career, even if the job is imperfect yet. But then there is a different job choice, one that was born out of necessity, and for whatever reason, that job was the best alternative at the time.

At some point, that person may decide to go back to school to improve their career or change careers altogether. I have met many students like this through my work as an educator. These students have become dissatisfied or unfulfilled in their jobs and recognized a need for change.

Amanda Morty

> *I had studied Fashion Designing at a prestigious fashion school in my state. Everyone had fought against it, especially my parents, because they could not comprehend earning*

> *money as a fashion designer. It sounded absurd to them, but I knew what I wanted, and that was to be a great fashion designer. I was willing to pick that as a career rather than get into one where I would wake up each day unhappy with myself. It was simply unbearable to even think of living that sort of life.*

My advice to young people, especially graduates who are just stepping into the labor market, is to not rush into things. One thing that should be known and understood is that there is a time for everything. You should never feel pressured simply because everyone expects you to have gotten your career at the start. You are entirely free to take your time and properly think about what you want to do and how to go about it.

It would be best to choose the career that makes you happy and not what pays the most in anything you do. Even having excess money does not often guarantee happiness at all. Ensure that you learn to pick your happiness over everything before taking steps into planning a career path. Whatever career path you take, you must do what suits you.

As Time Goes By

For the person who began with a definitive career plan, it is likely they will not consider other options until later in life, and their dream may stem from a need to do something different - whether it is a change of position or interest in finding a job that provides new meaning for them. For the person who has a job and then, over time, creates a career from it, or they have not found a clear path and frequently switch jobs, they will eventually begin to remember the dreams they once had.

However, those dreams may not align with their present job, or they may feel too far out of reach. But dreams do not need to be forgotten - and they can become a new career set point, provided they can be translated into something realistic and attainable. It takes roughly about ten years in any given profession before you become a professional at it.

Realizing Your Dreams

A dream perception is something you hope to achieve or a person you wish to become. It can consist of that nagging feeling that there is something more you want to do, but it has been set aside for some time. It may also be described as a calling or another job you could now have with a different career path. Either way, a dream causes you to feel unsettled at times - that there is something you have not yet completed. The following are some tools you can utilize to realize your dreams.

It might take some time to realize your dreams, but it is possible with the right efforts. As a young adult, especially one who is willing to be responsible, you can achieve all you set your mind to do.

This will be the right plan for young graduates to become what you envisage as the ideal adult. It is essential to understand some of the points discussed and watch how things would be for you when applying them, especially in your career.

Articulate Your Dream

Begin by talking through or writing out what you believe your dreams to be - and then try to write it out with specific details and include as many changes to it as you can remember. This will help you determine what is causing your feeling of wanting to do more and better understand any job dissatisfaction you may be experiencing now or have felt throughout your career.

Go Back to the Basics

See if you can remember what interested you as a child. Can you articulate a specific memory, and are you doing it now? If not, can you pinpoint when or how the interest was lost? The use of a quiet time journal can help you sort through your renewed thoughts over time and develop a clear picture of the interests you have had and the progress you have made along the way. This process will allow you to resolve any lingering feelings from the past and help you begin a forward focus.

Develop a Realistic Plan

If you find out that all through the process of self-reflection and self-analysis that there is something else you may enjoy doing or another path you would like to take, which goes beyond your present job, then it is time to establish a plan. As you formulate a plan, you will need to consider what you should do to prepare for a new job or career and then set both short-term and long-term goals. For example, consider if you will need to take a class, attend some form of training, or begin a degree program. This allows you to view your future from a position of professional development.

Balancing a Dream and a Job

Visions and dreams are the languages of the spirit, just like English is the language you speak; in a dream, you might be shown a picture or image to guide you for your pursuit. Having a dream is not being silly or acting like a child - although a child's imaginative state of mind certainly has merit. A dream is also more than a representation of an unfulfilled life. It is a desire to do more, grow in your career, and have new experiences. A dream is hopeful as it provides visualization of a goal you can develop. You can be a responsible adult, hold a job, be in a career, and still dream. It is an indicator that your job and employment do not have to become stagnant to you, now that you have an ideal image of an improved future for yourself.

You will find it useful to view your dreams as a source of hope and inspiration. Become inspired to develop a new plan for yourself and have fun as you expand your capacity to learn and capability to create new career goals. People who have forgotten about their dreams, or say they have none, also have not developed a clear vision of their future beyond what they are doing now. But that does not have to be you any longer as you become aware of a new future that you are in control of and have created from your dreams and career aspirations.

Here are five ways you can be a more responsible person:

1. If you have lost your job, do not break down. There are plenty of opportunities on this fertile earth. Surf the web and look where you fit in at the work front and start applying for jobs. Indeed, an excellent job will land on your lap. Give it a little time and be patient.
2. Look after your family through thick and thin. As the saying goes, united we stand; divided we fall. So, stick with your family, share family chores, and share your problems with them. Undoubtedly, several solutions for your issues will lurk up.
3. If you have issues and problems with a co-worker, brainstorm how you can ease their relationship. As it goes, make peace with all men as much as it lies within your power by firstly making peace with yourself; then you

can be at peace with others. Remove resistance. Go with the flow. Start taking it easy at work with all the people involved. Undoubtedly, your problems will start to dissolve only because you cared to take some responsibility for the case.

4. Your prime purpose on this earth is to have a fulfilled life and live the life God wants you to live. We live on earth for a period on probation to acquire life values for the real dwelling invisible to the naked eye for now. Make wise choices, and do not be hasty about them.

5. Do you have children who have become teenagers, and they have become rowdy? They do not listen to you and are incredibly bad-mannered. How do you handle such a situation? Mention it to God in prayer, listen to his counsel, and act on instructions you receive. Take a family vacation. Talk with your spouse about the problem. Discuss it in a family meeting. Discuss it lightly during holidays with your entire family. Reason with them and let them know you are disappointed in their current attitudes and what you expect from them. Remember,

persuasion is better than force. Make the problem lightly known to them and let them immerse in it and find themselves. Indeed, you will start to see them behave and talk in ways you would like them to do over a short period.

Financial Responsibility Tips

In this age of irresponsibility, in this time of finger-pointing, in this era of blaming everyone else for our ignorance - it is time to step up and be an adult who has an eye on the future yet enjoys the present without jeopardizing the foundations we all need and require.

It is time to be financially and emotionally responsible.

As much as it may be convenient to act surprised when people go into debt, it is nothing more than blind ignorance and massive irresponsibility that causes a lot of people to spend more than they earn and to want more than they need, whichever way we look at it, no matter what occurs to us, we should always look at the worst-case scenario before proceeding with any financial decision - whether that be the decision to have a child, buy a car, or take a vacation.

Mrs. James does not support lending people money, for her, the best she hoped for was to get her money back, and the probability was that she would lose her money and the friendship in almost all cases.

Think before spending, before buying too much that you do not need and do not use. Think. You owe nobody but yourself a financial responsibility.

If we look at all the possibilities and are prepared to take that risk, well then, it will be as it is, and the surprise is taken out of the equation, but the responsibility is not.

Here are some ways you can save money and be financially fit:

1. Develop a financial plan. Identify your long-term goals, save regularly and establish a budget. Make a list of the things you would want to achieve financially and review them from time to time.

Jonah had told himself that he wanted to be a millionaire before the age of 30. He started to make plans on how he would achieve this, and every step and decision he took financially was usually in line with this vision. Before he clocked 30, he already had a certain amount in his bank account that qualified him as a multi-millionaire.

2. Save. You are a hard-working young adult, so do not forget to pay yourself first. Set up a savings plan with your credit union or bank. If you can automatically get the savings deposited into your bank or credit union account without doing it yourself, it is easier to build your savings.

This is something I usually advise a lot of young adults, especially young graduates, to imbibe. Learning to save cannot be overemphasized. Set up a savings plan for yourself.

I had a friend called Josh. We graduated from college, and as young graduates, we were excited about finally starting our careers. We both got jobs and started working right away. While I always found a way to use up all the money once I received my paycheck, I never knew Josh was saving up.

Barely three years after we started working, Josh invited me over to his house-warming party. He had just gotten an excellent property in a great neighborhood. I was happy yet envious at the same time because I felt somewhat cheated.

*I spoke to Josh to let me in on his secret to such quick wealth, and he uttered one word to me, **"Save,"** and I was taken aback by that. I felt like he was not telling me everything, and I urged him to tell me more, but he laughed and repeated the same word.*

It turns out that Josh started saving 10 dollars every day. It was hard, but it was something he was willing to do. I had no idea that saving could go a long way in ensuring some sort of financial freedom. It had always been something I took with laxity.

3. Build an emergency safety net. Many financial advisors advise saving up to six months of living expenses in case of an emergency. If you cannot save six months of living expenses, start with one month's payments and regularly increase it. You can begin by stowing away one month's salary for an emergency period.

4. Got an Increase**? Raise** your savings! If you get a surge at work, immediately increase the percentage of your salary that goes into savings. You will not miss the extra money, and you will be growing your nest egg.

> *As I said, you can always save some more. There is no limit to how much you can save. If you were saving 500 dollars monthly, you could increase it to 700 dollars when you get a raise. All you must do is choose a savings plan that would be suitable for you financially.*

5. Manage and build your credit. When you take out a motor car loan or use your credit card, you are establishing credit. The appropriate way to build good credit is to pay your bills on time to prove you are responsible for managing your debt.

6. Pay bills on time. You can avoid late fees and high-interest payments, which can add up and make it harder to pay down the remaining balance. Settling accounts on time is noted and recognized by leading companies and institutions.

7. Read the fine print. Be sure to read, interpret and ask about interest rates and any additional fees when you apply for credit cards, loans, or lease an apartment.

8. Choose the right insurance plan. Whether it is for your health, car, apartment, or life, make sure you have the right coverage and indemnity to cover yourself and your funds.

9. Monitor your credit report. Credit scores are investigated when you apply for a job, buy a car, rent an apartment, etc. That is why it is good to monitor your credit report for any discrepancies or identity theft.

10. Being financially responsible is not just something that you do because others expect you to. You must be financially responsible as that is liberating.

Monitor your spending and watch the way cash flows in and out of your account. You can cut down on unnecessary expenditure and draft out a plan that lets you monitor and know the things your money goes into.

For example, you can draft out a bill like this for your monthly expenses based on your 7000-dollar salary a month.

Expenses for the month: Savings - $ 1000

Food - $1500
Other expenses and maintenance- $ 1700

This is just a rough draft of what you can do with your cash. Depending on how much you receive, you must plan what you spend your money on.

Being emotionally responsible is a dying art that few of us practice, and none of us are taught. Instead, we are lied to, 'miseducated,' and encouraged into the wrong frame of mind from the moment we are born.

We are pushed into a state of dependence instead of a life of independence; because of our childhood brain-washing, the stories we are fed, the movies we devour, and the insecurities we allow to permeate our lives, our relationships end up as emotional wrecks, and our search for love seems to consume us to the point of destruction; instead of us being responsible adults who work on the basis that we need a good foundation (filling your thoughts with the sayings of

Jesus) to build a substantial edifice and that foundation has to be made on an individual who understands themselves and is honest and forthright about their strengths and weaknesses; being reliant upon another human for emotional stability is an anomaly that makes no sense and does not work. We can only be liable for our own emotions.

CAREER

What is your profession? Forget about how you describe this to others for now and just think for a bit about how you define your career to yourself. What does it imply to you to have a career? Is it just your job? Is it something you do to make a living? Is it what you do for funds? Is it your work?

Most people would define a career as more than a job. Above and beyond a job, a career is a long-term work pattern, usually across multiple positions. A career implies professional development to build skills over a period, where one moves from novice to expert within a particular field. And finally, I would argue that a profession must be consciously chosen; even if others exert influence over you, you should still ultimately choose to become a lawyer, doctor, or accountant. If you did not make a conscious choice at some point, I would then say you have a job but not a career.

One of the difficulties I see many people experiencing lately is that they spend much of their days working at a job that is not part of a consciously chosen profession. Once you graduate from university or college and enter the workforce, you do not suddenly learn what kind of career to build. Most likely, you focus on getting a job as your first step after school. And you probably must make this choice in your early 20s. After a decade or two, you have established a work pattern and gathered up some expertise know-how. But at what point did you pause to ask, what is my profession going to be?

Many young adults, especially graduates, are usually quick to jump at any job they are offered without first thinking about the future, especially regarding the career path they want to take.

Sometimes when you question people what their profession is (instead of asking what their job is), the question makes them uncomfortable. Why? This is because they think of a career as intentionally chosen, purposeful, and meaningful, and they do not see those qualities in their trade. Another possibility is that they might feel deep down that their real profession or career lies elsewhere, often the case with most people. The jobs they are in are not the actual career path they should be on.

A countless number of us have been in that situation before, so we can relate to these things to some extent. *I remember one job I had taken simply because I felt the pay was good and I could be happy there. Fast forward six months, and I was already thinking of resigning because it was just not working. Deep down, I knew that was not the career I wanted. I just was not cut out for it.*

Just because you have been working in a field for many months or years does not mean you have to change that work pattern into your profession. The past is the past. You can continue to run the same way and follow that same path into the future, but at any time, you are also free to make a total break with the past and turn yourself onto an entirely new trade path in the future. Ask yourself if you were beginning over from scratch today, fresh out of school, would you still choose the same line of work? If the answer you give is no, you only have a job right now, not a career. Your career lies elsewhere.

Therefore, I would always emphasize that young graduates take their time before choosing the type of career they want to establish themselves. Like I would always say, there is absolutely no reason to rush because your success journey is different from those of others. Make decisions at your own pace and not because other people are already making major career moves. You should have a definite answer to specific questions before choosing the type of career you want to go into.

Think about this for a moment. What is the core of your profession? What is the bigger picture of what you do? What do you contribute? If you work for a big company, then how do your actions contribute to some larger purpose? Be honest with yourself. And do not ignore your company's role in your career; your career depends heavily on contributing to people on your down line. If you genuinely assign a noble purpose to what you do, that is great. For example, if you are working at a grocery store, you might be inspired by the fact that you help feed people. But do not force it if you do not believe it. If you feel your contribution is weak, uncertain, or even hostile, then admit that to yourself, even if you don't immediately plan to do anything about it.

Go behind the labels. Do not stop at defining your career as a computer programmer, lawyer, or doctor. What are you contributing to as a computer programmer? How does your job make a difference in other person's lives? Is it nothing more than a means for you to amass wealth and make money? As a lawyer, do you resolve disputes and spread peace, or do you milk conflict for cash? As a doctor or nurse, do you heal people, or are you just a lawful pusher? What is the essence or core of your line of work right now?

Now when you have your justification and answer, you next must ask yourself, is this you? Is this truly a field that reflects the best of who you are as a person, your talents, and your natural gifts, and you do it with little or no effort?

For example, suppose you see the real purpose behind your current work line as making a handful of children/youth wealthier in knowledge. In that case, nothing is nobler than that, then is that an exact reflection of your best input? Is that you?

If you already have a profession that accurately reflects the best of who you are, that is wonderful.

But if you do not, then realize that you are free to change it. Suppose your career as a regional distributor for a major soft drink manufacturer boils down to pushing sugar water to make people fatter. In that case, you don't have to preserve it in that form.

I assume that if you realize that your current work does not fit who you are, you must choose. You must decide if you deserve to have a career that truly suits you. If you do not feel you deserve it, you will settle for defining your career in such narrow terms as job, money, boss, coworkers paycheck, promotion, etc. No one is imposing on you to take that as your definition of a profession.

As a young graduate trying to find your career path in life, you must understand that it is most likely a lifelong decision, so think, ***do I want to be doing this for the next thirty years of my life? Would I be happy doing this in the next 30 years?*** Contrarily, you can choose to grasp or embrace another definition of a career that uses terms like purpose, assignment, calling, contribution, meaning, abundance, happiness, fulfillment, etc. This requires a top-down approach. You first pray to find out what you are created to be, do, and fulfill. Studying the scriptures helps find out your mission to the earth, what your purpose here is, what kind of contribution do you want to make with your life? Once you figure that out through seeking God in prayers, then you work down to the level of how to show and manifest that in terms of the work and tasks you do.

And for many people, the seeming impossibility of that manifesting part is paralyzing. This is especially true for men, who usually take their responsibility as breadwinners very seriously. You see yourself logically having two choices: You could stay in your current job, which pays the bills and earns you a good living, or you could jump into something that fits you better, but you just cannot see how to make it. You have a mortgage to pay and a family who depends on you; you cannot do that to them are all thoughts that come.

The complication is thinking that these are the only alternatives, assuming that you must choose between money and peace of mind or happiness. That theory or assumption is what causes the paralysis against the action. You can also foresee or envision the third alternative of having money and happiness together. That is the most likely outcome. If you do not currently have a deeply fulfilling career to yourself in the sense that you know you are contributing in a way that matters, then deep down, you will sabotage yourself from going too far with it.

You will always know that you are going on the wrong path, and this is going to pump a demotivating slump over everything you try to do in that line of work. You will do your job, but you will never feel that you live up to your potential. You will always have problems with procrastination and weak motivation, and they will never be resolved or solved no matter how many time management techniques you attempt. Your task or job will never feel like a truly satisfying career -- it just cannot grow into that because you have planted your career tree in lousy soil. You will always be cemented and stuck with a bonsai.

But when you get your line of work aligned from top to bottom, such that what you are ultimately contributing is an expression of the best of yourself, the resources will come too. You will be enjoying what you do so much, and you will find your work so fulfilling that turning it into an income stream will not be that hard. You will find a way to do it. Making resources is not at odds with your greater purpose; they can lie on the same path. The more resources you make, the greater your ability to contribute.

But most importantly, you will feel you deserve all the resources you earn. When your specialty or craft is aligned with the best of who you are, you will not secretly think that your continued career success means going farther down the wrong path. You will not hold back anymore. You will want to take your career as far as possible because it interprets who you are. And this will make you far more open-minded and more receptive to all the opportunities that are all around you, financial or otherwise.

But how do you make this transition? Is a leap of faith required? I think of it as more of a leap of courage, and it is a logical kind of courage, not an emotional one. It comes down to deciding how important your happiness and fulfillment are to you. How essential is it for you to have meaningful, fulfilling work that satisfies your mission on earth? Is it OK for you to continue and remain working in a field that does not allow you to add and contribute the very best of who you are? If you spot yourself in such a situation, then your answer is yes -- you have made it OK for you to endure and tolerate this position or condition.

But you see, self-actualizing persons who successfully make this leap will, at some point, conclude that it is not OK. It is intolerable. They rise and respond,

"Wait a minute here. This is unacceptable for me to be spending the bulk of my time at a job that is not a deeply fulfilling career. I cannot keep doing this. This ends now."

These people "wake up" by realizing that what is most vital about a work line is the high-level view or perception that includes happiness, fulfillment, and living on purpose. Things like money, success, and achievement are a very distant second. But when you work from within the first category, the second category takes care of itself.

Before you have had this awakening, you most likely did not see how that last sentence is possible. And that is because you do not understand that it is nothing more than a choice. You have probably picked to put money above fulfillment in your current line of work. That choice means that you will not have satisfaction. But it is not that you cannot have dignity -- you can select to change your preferences and act on them at any time. The natural selection you made was not to be fulfilled in your current line of work. You bought into the misconception that money is at odds with fulfillment and that money is the more important of the two, so that is all you see. No matter what job you take, you will find that this inference turns out to be genuine for you.

But once you get-up-and-go through the **"waking up"** experience and firmly decide to put fulfillment first, you suddenly realize that being fulfilled *AND* having plenty of resources is also a choice available to you. There are countless ideas for you to do both; you simply must permit yourself to see them. You will realize that you were the one who chose *EITHER-OR* instead of *AND,* while all the time, you were free to select *AND* pick whenever you wanted.

You set the code for your career choices. Most likely, your current average ranks fulfillment and meaningful contribution meager compared to working on exciting tasks and making sufficient resources. But those standards are yours to set. At any point, you are free to say, **"Having a significant and fulfilling career is an absolute MUST for me. Working for money alone is not an option."** And once you make this conscious selection, you WILL begin seeing the opportunities that fit this new standard. But you will never even recognize those opportunities if it remains OK for you to spend all your work time being unfulfilled.

This may not just be in terms of working for a higher authority. Even if you see yourself starting a career as an entrepreneur, you have to also focus on why you are going into that business line and what you stand to achieve in the long run. If you are reasoning or thinking of starting up a company simply because you want to make money, it is safe to say that you are on the wrong path. While making profits is the primary goal of every business entity, you also must think of the impact your business should have on the industry in which you are operating.

I want to drive home this point. Having a fulfilling work line that earns you plenty of resources does not require a leap of courage. It only requires a choice. You just must wake up one day and tell yourself that you deserve both and that you will not settle for anything less. It is not about finding the right job. A career is not something you see; it does not require someone to give you something. You are not at the mercy of circumstances.

A line of work is something you create, something you build and constitute. It means that the job or task you do each day is aligned with what you know to be your purpose; once you start doing this kind of work, even if for no pay initially, your self-esteem will grow to the point where you will become so resourceful and open to new opportunities that you will have no trouble making plenty of money.

By then, the money will not be that vital. It will just be some funds for you to do more of what you love.

WHEN SHOULD YOU BEGIN YOUR CAREER?

Maybe you think you should work between secondary/high school and university to explore and research the world of work. Maybe you should know and recognize what you want to study before going to university so that you have your career path established before you spend thousands of dollars/pounds on your education. Or maybe you should use your university years as the time to explore crafts and specialty options. Each person is uniquely different, and development does not have a smooth or straight path. Career development is no exception. What if I said your career development begins as soon as you learn to walk, talk, and imitate those around you? Would you think I am not making sense, or do you think this makes sense to you?

Specialty advancement is part of human development and improvement. It begins at childbirth and continues as you master or guru more and more skills throughout your life. Today is a different day. Years ago, an individual would decide on a line of work and stay working for twenty to forty years in the same profession for their entire working life. Today, it is not unusual for individuals to change their specialty two or even three times in their working years. Line of work advancement and development does not move forward in a straight line. You need time to understand who you are, what you enjoy, what interests you, what you feel are your strengths and weaknesses, and what kind of lifestyle you want to live. All these things take time to explore, evaluate, and plan. This takes years! When do you begin? You began at birth!

> *Mrs. Bright, my friend, used to joke that her daughter was forty since she was four years old. As a young child, she showed traits and characteristics that could be considered and*

expressed career skills. She liked to be in charge, so you perceive that she would be a leader and a take-charge kind of person since she was four. She also loved to help others. She was the eldest of her three children and loved to help her younger sister and brother with whatever they were doing. She was a born leader, a teacher, a helper, a service-oriented type of personality. She knew very early that whatever career path she chose would include working with people, offering some help to others, being in charge, and believing she would be in some type of teaching capacity. As her daughter went through school, she was an excellent and hardworking student. In Middle School, it became clear that she was very good at Science, and she had a remarkable work ethic. When she got to secondary/high school, it was very evident that she was a great science student. During her daughter's sixteenth year, one of her best friends got a type of meningitis that caused her to be unable to speak or move. She was trapped in her own body. Mrs. Bright's daughter watched her friend relearn to use her body. She was deeply and passionately affected by this trauma for her friend. She became interested in the professionals that helped bring her friend back to being a fully functioning person after months and months of rehabilitation. Today, her daughter is an occupational therapist. She could enter university, knowing precisely what she wanted to study, and chose a line of work path that she had been developing since she was a young child.

So, when should you begin to think about a career path? Whether you know it or not, you have been thinking about and developing a career path since you were a small child playing house, playing roles, playing sports, playing an instrument, drawing, singing, building models, listening to music, solving puzzles, playing word games, playing maths games, trying to figure out how things work.

Contrary to what people think, starting your career does not start from a certain 'mature' age. You subconsciously start to prepare for it as soon as you have identified what it is you want to be or do.

Unlike Mrs. Bright's daughter, who knew what she wanted to do from a very tender age, some people usually have no idea what they want till they are well over 30! For these people, they must think and ponder for a long time on what they want to become before finally making a final choice/decision.

Herbert was 32 years and a graduate of Communication Studies from college and had already spent seven years working in an advertising industry before realizing he was on the wrong career path. He enjoyed his work line, but he knew that he couldn't keep at it for a long time. Herbert wanted to be a media personality, which was what he had always wanted to be. Was it too late for him to give off his career? It was not because he soon quit his job and finally started as a small-time radio presenter.

All these activities and actions involve skills you have developed along the journey of your life. Pay attention and consideration to how you spend your time. What do you do in your spare time? What actions or behavior do you take each day that you enjoy? Do you enjoy working with individuals? Do you enjoy working and engaging with data and information? Do you enjoy fixing things, building stuff, making kinds of stuff work? What activity truly interests you?

When you have a couple of hours or days to yourself, what do you do with that time? What brings you fulfillment and enjoyment? Satisfaction? Contentment? What challenges you in a way that stimulates you rather than frustrates you? What activities bring a smile to your face?

When you can answer these questions, ask yourself what careers can offer me these enjoyable opportunities. You will have to work for many years of your life. If you work to earn a salary, your days will be long, tough, and challenging. It would help if you were capable of engaging in work for satisfaction in what you do. You need to be able to feel and sense content in your workplace. You want to enjoy and relish what you do. You want to feel optimistic about what you do, enjoy what you do, and appreciate the wages or that it provides you. You also want to afford the lifestyle that equates.

So, think back over your life or essence and focus on the activities that brought you satisfaction, contentment, and joy. You could be seventeen, twenty-seven, or sixty-seven. Your life experiences have been valuable learning or schooling experiences. Think back to scrutinize and explore your history. If you enjoy working and engaging with people, find a social career. Maybe you want to help others. Explore and research the many medical occupations and see if any of them fit. Perhaps you would love to teach young people and help them develop their minds and skills through education. Maybe you would enjoy and relish business fields where you help people build and run successful businesses.

Maybe you love working with your hands. Perhaps you have always been fascinated by cars and would love to learn how to fix an engine. Perhaps you have always been interested in electricity and would relish being an electrician. If you love working with your hands, then find a career that allows you to satisfy this need in you, releasing the life and light in you to your environment.

Maybe you have always loved being creative. You have loved to tell stories or draw pictures or build things. Perhaps you would love to write, design, or construct buildings. If you are creative, utilize your creativity. Write, draw, design, dance, create, and play music, build, and create. Nurture, nourish, and develop your talents. Nurture your strengths. Be who you are in your character, heart and turn it into your career.

ADULT ATTITUDE ADJUSTMENT

As adults, there are times where everything seems to go wrong, and it just feels like the world is against us. Got a bad hair day, your boss yelled at you because you made a mistake in the PowerPoint presentation, your car broke down when you were already late for an appointment, etc.

All these things make you want to yell, and you find yourself complaining about the thousand ways your life is falling apart, which further sinks you into depression. Anyone who steps in your path becomes a victim of your boiling tantrums.

Suddenly, you find yourself yelling at everyone, you become apathetic, and you start to appear cold to even the people that matter, but at the end of the day, just one question is on your mind, and that is, *"why is all of this happening to me?"*

We all should understand as adults that our attitudes affect our behavior and the way we view things, which, in turn, influences how we communicate with the people around us. The bitter truth is that we sometimes like to blame the circumstances affecting us as the reason why we act in a certain way. It is not always right.

The thing is that sometimes we just have a bad attitude. This is a hard pill to swallow, right? Unfortunately, this is the truth that we most times like to avoid. This is because when you have a bad attitude, you attract negative things to yourself. A negative attitude attracts and produces adverse outcomes, so that difficult time you are passing through might result from your mindset if you take time to look at things constructively.

Of course, there would be signs that would arise that will make you realize that you require an attitude adjustment, and what are some of these signs?

You frequently have the same issues with others.

At times like this, you find yourself being triggered by a particular thing that people do. It sets you off, and you start up a quarrel with them, but the problem might not be them but you. When you continuously have issues with other people because of a particular subject, then it is a sign that you might need an attitude adjustment.

You are never wrong

You never consider the fact that you might be wrong. To you, others are wrong, and you are always right. You think that others need an attitude adjustment and not you.

At this point, you always believe others do not know what they are doing and that only you have the right answer to everything. This is another sign that you must self-adjust your attitude.

> *I once knew someone like this. He was an acquaintance, and I had to hang out with him sometimes because he was a friend. I noticed from most of the discussions we had because he always felt he was right and made everyone's opinion feel wrong.*

It was often discovered that he was wrong, but he never accepted even when the facts were right there in his face.

You always complain about things

When you find yourself always nagging and continually complaining about the things happening in your life, you find yourself being bitter, and this can be dreadful and tiring for the people around you, and that is bad.

People would start to avoid you because they are tired of listening to you throw tantrums about how bad your life is going. You begin to lose friends at times like this because you now appear to be a bitter person.

If you are guilty of this, you must admit that you need an adult attitude adjustment.

All of these and others are just some of the signs that show just how much the problem is with you and not others, and the quicker you are to accept that you need an attitudinal adjustment even as an adult, the more manageable for you.

Now that you might have accepted that your attitude might be the problem, *what are you willing to do about it?* That is where the term ***Adult Attitude Adjustment (AAA)*** comes in.

As an adult in need of an attitude adjustment, there are certain things you need to practice if you want to become a better person and attract positive things to yourself.

First, you must understand that while there might not be a lot that humans can control, we do have control over our attitudes and behaviors. It would be best if you believed that only you have the power to change the things going on in your life, and one of them is needing to accept an attitudinal change. You can control your emotions and how you react to things.

Another thing you must do is to have a **positive mindset.** Nothing surpasses the power of positive thinking. Positive thinking has the potential to turn things around for you once you have mastered the ability to think a good thought.

> *My grandfather was a happy person, and it usually baffled everyone in my family. Even when things were tough and every other person felt sad, Grandpa would walk around humming a tone with a cheerful smile on his*

face. Sometimes it used to piss my mum off because she thought he was merely inconsiderate and not empathetic, but that was not true.

I discussed with him just some years before he died, and I asked why he was always happy. He had said that the reason for his sunny attitude was because he had told himself that he was still going to be positive no matter what happened. Even when bad things happen, he would brush it off and go on with his life. In his words, **'life's too short to be caught, not smiling.'**

That was, by far, the most important lesson I had ever learned in my life.

Your thoughts affect your perception of things and how you would respond to things. When you think about good things, you will find yourself in a good disposition, which generally affects your mood for the day and sets you in a perspective that attracts positive outcomes. It would be best if you understood that once you master the art of positive thinking and possessing a positive mindset, not only does it do wonders for you, it attracts other people to you.

Once you have mastered the power of having a positive mindset, **kindness** comes to you naturally. We cannot begin to overemphasize the importance of being kind to people. Being kind to yourself and others is just another step towards a wholesome attitude adjustment.

Another way to adopt the right attitude is to **identify the emotions** that make you act the way you do. Make sure you understand the feelings that get you easily frustrated and learn to control them. It is crucial for you as an adult to have total control over your emotions because these emotions also greatly influence our thoughts, behavior, and attitudes we portray. Therefore, it is necessary to have a firm hold on your feelings and how you react to them.

Another thing to do is to learn to **admit your mistakes.** This shows a deep sense of humility that cannot be rivaled. Once you are willing to admit your mistakes, it becomes easier to say the word 'sorry,' and you must understand that you cannot always be right.

You must understand that many bad things can happen. You must learn to **accept that things will not always be right.** Adulthood comes with its ups and downs, and while good things would happen, be prepared for the worse and accept that many bad things would occur.

The fact is, there are a lot of adults who are in dire need of an attitude adjustment, but they do not know this, so they walk around with a bad attitude, which makes them appear toxic to others. For these adults, there are a lot of things that need to be learned.

You need to identify these traits that need attention and then work on becoming a well-adjusted adult.

THINGS YOU SHOULD KNOW ABOUT YOURSELF

*I*t is essential to have a career plan. This will help you oversee the direction of your career. It will also inform you of the craft skills and knowledge you will need and plan how you may acquire them. One vital element in the development of a career plan is self-assessment. Self-evaluation is crucial because it leads to self-understanding.

Anything you choose to do takes about seven to ten years to start flourishing and be fruitful, so stay at it.

Knowing yourself from your maker's point-understanding is often missing in our day and age. Notwithstanding, this was no less true at the times of the older generation than it is today. How, then, does one arrive at such knowledge? You wonder. This book aims precisely to answer this very question.

Again, the process of arriving at an understanding is a self-assessment. A self-assessment is an honest conversation with your inner being about yourself on what God created you for and to be. It will often assist you in including it in that conversation with other people who know and care about you. Such a process will lead to discovering things about yourself that you might not have been aware of. If you wish to make sure that you plan your work line appropriately, you need to know the kind of person you are.

A line of work strategy needs not to be too complicated. How sophisticated, refined and detailed you want to be is entirely up to you. Nonetheless, a sound self-assessment will consider, among others, the following aspects of your life: your values, your passion, your life path, your goals in life, and your current knowledge. Let us now look at each one of these briefly.

Your Values.

Everyone has some things they consider more important than anything else in life. These are things they would likely always stand for, no matter the circumstances. These things could be some social aspects of life (like family), some political convictions (like women's right to vote), some scriptural doctrines, etc. Generally, values are things for which someone would even consider dying. *For example, Nelson Mandela believed that apartheid was unjust and, in his own words, admitted that he was prepared to perish to see that political system collapse.* Whether they are mindful of them or not, everyone has values and ideals. You should know yours and take them into scrutiny when you plan your line of work and professional direction.

Your Passion/Zeal.

We all have things that we are zealous or passionate about. These are the things we enjoy. They are things we catch ourselves acting on all the time. In a way, we are never bored or tired of doing something we are passionate about. For example, some people enjoy reading. They read all the time, and they do it effortlessly. Others enjoy public speaking. They find great joy and an immense sense of accomplishment when they are vocalizing to a live gathering. Wherever they are, they instantly become the life of the conference. People's passions also keep them awake at night. If you pay attention to your inward being, you will discover what your desires are. They are things which easily excite you. When you are passionate or desirous about something, you always find a way to chat about it, and you can do that for a full day. Your passions should be factored into your work line plan.

Your Life Path

If you do not know and see where you are going, you can end up anywhere!

Create a compelling vision and practice daily to see beyond your struggles. Use positive thinking to help you stay on track and take action so you can see your dream come to life. Day by day, you create your future, make it one that you love, one where you can look back and be proud of your story.

Your Goals in Life

"If you do not perceive where you are going, any lane will get you there."

— LEWIS CARROLL

If you do not have any goals in life, other people will

create them for you. It is not enough to just set goals. You must take the necessary steps to make them a reality.

What do you want to achieve? What are the steps to getting there?

Your Current Knowledge

We all have some knowledge of specific areas. We may have to get such knowledge from previous studies or personal experiences. Sometimes we forget that we have such ability because we take it for granted. However, it is always good for you to think of all the assets (cognitive and others) you already have at your disposal. It does not particularly matter how you got them.

An essential thing is a fact that you do. As a unique bank puts it in a commercial, you may be wealthier than you think. Because of a lack of consciousness of what we already have, sometimes we spend a lot of time, cash, and energy building new foundations when we should build on foundations we already have in place.

> *I recently took a ride with a friend of mine to a conference. As we were talking along the way,*

I got to know her a little more. I learned that her parents were farmers. My colleague referred to herself as a farm girl. She also mentioned some of her childhood friends who, like her, were also farm girls. She was raised, grew up on a dairy farm, and learned farming from her parents. Later, when she went to university, she took agriculture.

After her studies, she went back to the farm and worked for her parents. As her parents were aging, she got more and more control of the family business. Of course, later, her parents retired, and she got full control. At this point, she managed to grow the farm by buying more land.

Today she is a considerably wealthy woman. During and after this conversation, I could not help but realize how this woman built on something she already had at her disposal. It might have taken her more work to be as successful as she has been if she chose to follow a different career path, like, for example, politics.

RELATIONSHIP

As adults, the two most important things that are a consistent part of our lives are our careers and our relationships. This is because they go hand in hand in shaping our lives and our future.

When we talk about relationships, we are talking about love and courtship in this context. As young and emerging adults, relationships are a constant in our lives. We are at the mark or point in our lives where we continuously crave attention and love, which leads us to always seeking to start a relationship with someone we think could make us happy.

There are simply two types of relationships people can end up with: **Positive** and **negative connections**.

Relationships are part of adulthood, and it is a criterion for developing and establishing social relationships, among others. It brings about a sense of identity that is important for adults, especially among emerging adulthood. Sometimes, these relationships can be long-lasting, and at other times, they end up sourly. Why, then, are relationships meaningful as part of maturity?

Tina Stone

I grew up in a loving home where I was the only child and had both parents' love and attention. For sixteen years of my life, I thought I had the ideal family till one afternoon, I got back from school and saw my mother crying. My parents were getting a divorce because they both were unhappy with each other.

My whole world was shattered, and I felt betrayed for a long time because I felt I had been living a lie. That, in a way, changed how I viewed relationships, and for a long time, I did not see the need to get into one. Even while in college, I had flings, but I never wanted anything serious to do with anyone. I always thought of my parents, and the thought that usually came to my mind was, ***why are relationships so important to people knowing that they would both end up hurting?***

Relationships are an essential aspect and part of growing up to be responsible adults and, in the long run, prepare us for marriage and parenthood. Relationships are critical for young adults because they significantly influence our self-esteem and bring about a sense of belonging.

Sadly, a lot of young people are satisfied with being in toxic relationships nowadays. They prefer the type of relationship that thrives on public attention, sex, and other unhealthy vices. Nobody wants to spend time having a quality type of relationship that is value-driven, and that is where the problem starts. We should all strive for a healthy relationship.

A healthy relationship can boost one's confidence and promote overall physical and mental health and improve social skills. In contrast, a problematic relationship can hurt a person's emotional, psychological, and even physical health, making one very unhappy.

A positive relationship builds everyone for the future by improving and encouraging each other to solidify and maintain long-lasting friendships with people outside the relationship.

A positive relationship has the following benefits to both partners, and they are:

- A positive relationship acts as a support mechanism for couples because they can seek support from their partners, especially during hard and challenging times.

I cannot help but feel comfortable whenever I speak to my friend about certain things, especially when it comes to emotional issues affecting me. She has a way of comforting me with her words. It is like she is a guardian angel of some sort. And to be honest, I do not know what I would do without her sometimes.

— OWEN

- A positive relationship also inspires one to seek personal growth. When you are honest and healthy, your partner usually encourages you to achieve your own goals and objectives. A good relationship seeks individuals to flourish and have their accomplishments.

I always knew I was a good writer, but I lacked the confidence to go ahead and own a blog, one of my life-long dreams. However, I had to tell my friend about it, and he encouraged me to start up a blog and even pursue a career as a professional writer. It was so beautiful how he believed in me and that alone made me want to do my best. Today, I own my blog, and I am a professional writer for others. I would never have been ever able to do all of this without the encouragement of my friend.

— LEANNA

- Another benefit of seeking a healthy and positive relationship is that it rubs off on others around and extends to your immediate circle. A positive relationship influences not just you but also your family and friends and how you relate with them.

My son used to be a very temperamental child while growing up. Billy could get angry over the littlest of things, and being with him was like walking on eggshells because you never knew when he could switch and become an angry 'beast.'

One summer vacation, he showed up at the family dinner with a pretty girl he introduced to us as his friend. It was intriguing because she looked so fragile that we did not think she would be able to stand any of Billy's tantrums.

However, we were shocked to see that Billy no longer reacted to things the way he used to because she had a way of calming him down in ways we never could. Suddenly, being with him was not such a scary thing as we now rest assured that we could crack a joke around him without unleashing a whirlwind of angry emotions.

— BETTY

- A positive relationship offers both partners an opportunity to do all that they want to do, therefore adding meaning and purpose to the lives of both parties involved. It brings about a stronger sense of identity and gives every action you take an extra meaning.

I have had the most fantastic experience with my friend. Every day we learn new things about each other. Everything is so beautiful and effortless with her. I could say that I am blown away by someone who once did not believe in me, and the help I get when I am with her is something I will always cherish.

— CLINTON

- A positive relationship enables you to be more accountable to your partners. In turn, it allows you to build and showcase a level of responsibility and accountability to others around you, especially family members.

Being with my friend of five years, it already feels like I am a married man. I know that sounds hilarious, but that is how I think. It is like I am now programmed towards being responsible and accountable to her and my family.

Every decision I take is something I do while bearing her emotions and contribution in mind. She has shaped me to be a more responsible young man, and I must acknowledge that she is incredible. Do not be put off by what people say. There is still something nice about being in a relationship.

— BARRY

Relationships among adults can be exciting as well as challenging too. Some issues may sometimes arise in these relationships, and most of them are bordered on sex, one-sided relationships, cheating, and other insecurities that may play out among partners.

However, we should understand that these issues can be avoided, but finding different ways to sort these issues out if they do happen is essential. One of the best ways to go about this is through **effective communication.** Learn to talk things out with your partner and trash whatever issues you have. Always learn to talk things out. It brings about a level of understanding and tolerance among both partners.

Another way is by developing **mutual respect**. When in a relationship, one must respect their partner's ideas and input in whatever they discuss or embark on. Consideration is one of the essential attributes of a positive relationship, and both individuals need to realize and value this factor.

A healthy and positive relationship cannot stand without trust. **Trust** is the most significant deciding factor in any relationship, and individuals need to develop confidence in their relationship with each other. Everyone who has been in a long-lasting relationship can attest that trust is the most incredible foundation of any relationship.

Recently, this trend among young people feeling the need to show off their social media relationship. They want people to tag them as the 'picture perfect' couple. While this is not such a terrible idea, a relationship that thrives on social media has a very high probability of breaking than one that is out of the public's eyes. You must understand that once you start to view and listen to people's opinions on how your relationship should be, unknowingly, you begin to streamline whatever actions you take in your relationship, according to these public opinions.

You do not have to be swayed by what people put up before you. No relationship is ideal or perfect, and there is no relationship without issues. Quarrels are bound to occur, but it is essential to **be mindful** of the things we say to each other.

Contrary to popular belief, words do have a massive influence on how the relationship plays out. Words can make or break a relationship, so it is necessary for friends always to mind the words they utter to themselves, especially in a heated argument, because these words have a way of sticking and setting the victim off.

Relationships will always be a part of growing up. These will shape us and supply us with the experiences we need to know, primarily as they concern our emotional maturity. Therefore, young adults need to understand how these relationships work and how they will benefit them before venturing into one.

These emotional experiences we get from relationships are usually geared towards preparing us for marital life and coping with the challenges to come. Relationships can be a horrifying experience for everyone, especially when you get into a toxic and negative one. It can scar you, but it is geared towards teaching lessons, and we all must aspire to make all our relationships positive relationships. And this shouldn't just be with friends, but in the work/social relationships we have with other people.

We cannot talk about young adulthood without talking about relationships, managing their emotions, and even treating their relationships. Some individuals have been so affected by their previous relationships that they unconsciously offload these negative emotions on their new relationship. It is not supposed to be that way.

For a long time, I was an extremely wary fiancée *who never trusted her* fiancé *because I thought he would cheat one day. My previous relationships always had, for some weird reason ended with the guy cheating on me.*

When I got into this new relationship, I was very skeptical about his activities and was always alert whenever I saw his phone ring or when he told me he was going out with friends. Of course, I have never openly confronted him about it, but I fed off on my paranoia, and it started to affect our relationship. It was only when he threatened to break up with me that I realized that I needed to work on myself. Together we have both been to a counselor, and I do not always feel that way anymore. And with each day, I am learning to let go of past experiences and spare my partner the trouble.

— CATHERINE

The relationship is not about sex or what you define as love. Relationships are the stepping ground in which you can become a better person and, most importantly, a better husband or wife.

Therefore, young people need to model other positive relationships around them, especially close family members.

BALANCING CAREER AND
RELATIONSHIP

Time. There never seems to be enough.

There are relationships, career, personal interest, family, and social demands, all screaming for attention in our life. All of us have the same amount of time available to us as we begin a new day. Twenty-four hours to use or abuse as we see fit.

This is not a book about time management. Time management is a misnomer. You cannot manage time. Time passes, oblivious to your needs, desires, problems, goals, expectations, and dreams. You can only manage a variety of activities and attitudes within a framework of passing the time. Well, if we cannot manage time, what can we handle? We can control our resources, decisions, thoughts, expectations, challenges, people, failures, activities, successes, risks, feelings, goals, money, emotions, and a whole host of attitudes.

Let us get to the heart of the issue. Many people live with daily frustration, unable to effectively manage some or all the items on the previous list. They are anxious, troubled, and often angry at the relentless passage of time-insensitive to their wishes, demands, frustrations, and goals.

Many of these people feel stuck, have given up, or have settled, thinking, this is just the way it is and must be. They see themselves as a pawn to the demands and expectations of one or more areas of their life, therefore, robbing themselves of the pleasure and happiness available to everyone who has learned to live with balance.

These people are out of balance, and they know it. They feel like their life is out of control. They feel stuck. They see themselves with very few options. They do not realize that the choices that they have made in the past determine their next opportunities. Because of poor decisions in the present, there will also be equally limited options for a better future. Yes, we all always have choices, but if these choices are made with a narrow vision of what can be, an unclear picture of reality, or clouded perceptions and interpretations of people and circumstances, they will always be made with limited resources and understanding.

These people remain stuck. Some have moved on in some areas of their life, but they still feel unable to shed the feelings of anxiety that there is more to do, more to become, more to have, and more to learn, and not enough time to do it.

Several significant areas in a person's life demand a portion of their available time. They are family, career or business, social, personal development, spiritual development, physical development, personal interests or hobbies, friends, misc. Social activities, and let us not forget time to sleep and eat.

Is it possible to live a balanced life? Is it possible to satisfy the expectations of how we should be using our time? Is it possible to have it all? Become it all? Do it all? See it all? Learn it all? Read it all? No, it is not that kind of world.

So, we are back to a choice. How each of us decides to use or spend our time is an individual matter? Juggling the expectations of a boss, customers, spouse, children, parents, friends, siblings, and the world, in general, is a challenging and delicate task at best. No one has all the answers or easy formulas to this complicated life issue, but as the bible has it all, we only need to use it as our life manual and apply the instructions we get as we daily discover the right path. You will not find all answers in this book. What I hope you will find, however, is some insight or discovery as to why you feel as you are—the courage to modify any behavior or attitudes that are sabotaging one or several areas of your life.

You may have noticed that when one area of your life is out of harmony or balance that it impacts every other place as well. When you are devoting too much time (and only you know what is too much) to your career, every other aspect of your life is impacted. Every part of your life is intricately entwined with every other area. If you choose to devote no time to your personal growth, you will lack the skill, understanding, or wisdom to contribute positively to some other aspect of your life. By the same token, if you spend time regularly relaxing or meditating, it will help you find the patience or calmness that you will bring to your career or family issues.

Why do people get out of balance?

Several causes include but are not limited to:

unrealistic goals or a lack of goals, lack of planning, a need for approval and acceptance, inadequate personal growth, overestimation of abilities or skills, the inability to say no, the desire to please, lack of discipline, arrogance, greed, insensitivity, lack of spiritual development, un-managed ambition, the need for power, unchecked egos, lack of commitment and a lack of unity or integrity. Hefty list. I would guess that everyone who is out of balance in their lives is guilty of several of them. Being out of balance in life does not feel right.

Life is lived in the present, one moment at a time. It is not lived yesterday or tomorrow, but now. Every time you decide to spend time in a certain way, like spending time reading this book, you have eliminated all other choices of time used now. Once you choose to go to a movie, you have eliminated the options of dinner, dancing, golf, and so on. Once you decide to work late, you have chosen to sacrifice something else. I do not mean to be hilarious, but you cannot be in two places at once. You cannot be on vacation and at work too, although many people try. Once you choose one restaurant for dinner, you have eliminated all others for that meal.

People need to understand that they have choices and that their choices and consequences are a part of the bargain. Frustration sometimes sneaks into people's lives when they believe it is possible to break the rules, have it all, do it all, or become it.

You chose your career and life path. You chose your current relationship. You chose your current circumstances by the previous choices you have made. You made them for yourself. Even if you are in a career that was chosen for you by your parents (and that happens less and less today than years ago), you have chosen to stay in it even if you are unhappy. You have given the power in your life over to someone else.

If you rationalize that you must work eighty hours a week and weekends because your boss or organization expects it, you have given up your power to someone else. Then you might say, but I need this job or career. I need the money. No, you have chosen to need it. You could have chosen a different, more modest lifestyle that would have required less income. Like it or not, you are where you are because of your choices in every situation in life. Do you want a better life? Then you must make different choices.

I would like to share fifteen ideas with you that may help you put balance back into your life to find time for the people and goals in your life that are possibly being shortchanged, including yourself.

1. Spend some quiet time reflecting on the quality of your life in general. Not just a single area, but consider every aspect and the relationship of each to your overall life.
2. Make a list of all the areas or people in your life coming up short and why.
3. Determine which area of your life is getting most of your time and energy and which is getting the least. Ask yourself why. Is the gain in one place worth paying the price of a loss in another area? Only you can answer that question, and only you will pay the price or enjoy the rewards.
4. Write a letter to yourself about how you would like your life to look six months from now. Describe how you spend your time and what proportions of time are dedicated to your life's various activities and people.

5. Give yourself at least thirty minutes a day for thirty days to reflect on your overall life goals and your progress toward them.
6. Write a personal mission statement. Include your life values, guiding principles, desired outcomes, and the overall direction you want your life to take.
7. Move ahead mentally to age 70. What have you accomplished, what do your relationships look like, who have you become, and what is important to you? Now work backward. What do you need to change to get to where you would want to be? Remember, you have to change the quality of your future in the present.
8. Ask several people who know you well and be honest and nonjudgmental to offer feedback on your life and its direction. Listen and learn with an open and receptive attitude. You may not change because of the feedback they give you, but the insight you gain can give you some ideas that could be life-changing.
9. Take a few days off from your job, career, and current relationships. Spend time in a place that you are at peace and alone. It

could be the beach, the mountains, or anywhere where you can spend quality time with yourself evaluating your life without the distractions and expectations of others. Go with no agenda other than a discovery.

10. If you do not keep a journal of your thoughts, lessons learned, life progress, feelings, interests, or observations, start one today. Take a few minutes at the end of each day recording whatever you feel in some way contributed to who you are, how you think, and whom you are becoming in character.

11. Develop an action plan to re-allocate your time and energy to those people or activities important to you.

12. It is unnecessary to sell your business and quit your job to find a better balance in your life. It requires a conscious awareness of what your life is really like, a desire to modify it somehow, the courage to change, the necessary skills, and the commitment to stick with it.

13. Learn to detach from other people's emotional and or physical hold over you. It will not be easy. There will be people who use blame, guilt, manipulation, or any

number of emotional or biological techniques to keep you stuck in past behavior or thought patterns. They will know how to push your buttons, hoping to control you in some way. When you permit others to manipulate you in any way, you give them power over your life. Detachment means letting go of the hold other people have over you. You can still love them and want to be with them, but you no longer must be a slave to their "stuff."

14. Don't try and change everything over-night. It takes time to change attitudes and behavior that have developed over the years. One thing that changed the earth initially was when God spoke to it, and it is still the same way our lives can be turned around when God's word says to our lives. Be patient and loving with yourself. But you must also hold yourself accountable. Letting yourself off the hook or making excuses will not put you on the road back to a balanced life.

15. Reward your effort. Treat yourself when you achieve a "worked for" result. Make it something symbolic or significant, but whatever it is, make sure you take time to bask in the sunshine of success. Then begin

again. Do not spend too much time basking, or you may fall back into your old habits. Change, permanent change requires vigilance and persistence. You cannot let up until you have achieved total and permanent success. It will always be possible to fall back, so even though you have reached your goal, do not become too casual or relaxed. There will be new people and circumstances lurking in the shadows for a vulnerable moment. Be watchful.

None of these steps may be easy. Only you can decide if the potential outcome of more balance and inner peace is worth the price that must be paid. Do not change because of guilt, other people's expectations, or some casual or superficial whim. If you like working twenty hours a week and seeing your kids every day for a few hours. Fine. If you want to change, that is fine too. But do it for healthy convictions, emotional or physical reasons, not ego-driven motives.

FALLING IN LOVE WITH A CAREER YOU DO NOT HAVE

It is not just relationships that are unrequited. Some are spiritual and purely based on ambition and passion. A perfect example is falling in love with a career that you do not have.

Busy people spend at least eight hours per day all over the whole week. Perhaps you might be going to school for the same duration. Employed individuals and students who are always busy with activities that they need to do. Because of this, you might think of a job that you have wanted to achieve for so many years now. This excessive infatuation level might not even help you reach that dream job, but instead, it distracts you from success.

The question is, how can you address this potentially-breaking situation? Here are a few precise actions you can do if you are in love with a job you do not have.

Recognize what makes you demotivated.

If you have enjoyed your work or school time before, but now you wake up in terror of walking out of the house, consider the possible reasons you feel demotivated. Maybe you have had something going on with your life in your household, and it is going to make your job difficult. You might be working so hard. Still, it sounds like it is getting overlooked.

If you felt obsessed with a job that you have always wanted, ask yourself. You might think it is challenging to make every morning and know if you will be searching for a brand-new career tonight. However, before you offer your notice, try to explain what makes you mad – are you getting bored, demotivated, or feeling something even more profound?

Create a list of drawbacks

Consider what you should do with them to change the condition or fix the dilemma. Create another set of new projects to get them to partner with you. Hold them as a list of the little improvements you would like to see, and then start going on them or speak to somebody who might be willing to listen and assist you.

Actively alter what worries you

When you understand what makes you sad, you will pinpoint the core of the problem. Over the summer months, we all slip into unproductivity. For example, while other colleagues are on break, looking out at the bright outdoors, pinching an ice-cold pint in the garden. No one wants to go to work at this period. Yet we must pay the bills, and we need to show up. So, if you are upset at your workplace, you should be looking out for how you can make a difference.

Take a well-deserved rest

Give yourself a break. Take a well-deserved rest after a stressful week. Book a vacation, take a few days to hang out, or go for a short staycation, and make sure to reflect on you from your maker's perspective. Feel free to turn off your email alerts, and set aside all your work-related feelings for a while. Enjoy your day-off, and that will likely make you feel refreshed.

The outcome of getting obsessed with a job that you do not have is inconsistency. So, as a career aspirant, consider the recommendations mentioned above to avoid rushing things. Planning before taking any action always pays off.

HOW TO DEAL WITH CHANGES IN LIFE

The one constant thing in life is change. That does not mean we get used to it or fully embrace it, though. Several adults have grown to become unchanging, considering their mindsets. Many graduates would have conditioned their perspectives on what they should expect from society- job, housing, car, etc. immediately after they graduate. But when such did not come as expected, they end up committing suicide or losing their lives to depression and worries, culminating in them becoming mentally unstable.

After Stan graduated from university, he anticipated that he should get called up for an interview. A few months before his graduation, he had had his resume submitted in various establishments. Weeks strolled by, and nothing came forth from those establishments. He felt they might have forgotten though he was told, then they would get back to him.

His endless wait amounted to nothing. Weeks became months and months gradually became years. As all these continued, a pile of pressure gathered on him, and all he could think of was **SUICIDE**.

What do you think was responsible for Stan's death? Do you think it was the job that was not forthcoming? No! He was the architect of his predicament, and he knew he failed in that regard. What was that supposed to mean? He was not evolving with society. He believed the community was a ready-made environment that will hand over to him whatever his desires were. He underestimated the power of his ability to think and create something out of nothing.

When life does not give you what you demand, that is a change. Thus, you need to understand that life itself wants you, at that very moment, to change the situation around. Remember, opportunity does not come to you by chance or luck. You create an opportunity for yourself.

Had Mark Zuckerberg dropped out of Harvard only

to fall prey to the hands of depression, he would not have stunned the world today as the youngest billionaire from his creation of Facebook. Another person would have achieved that feat, and that would have amounted to loss on his part. Think outside of the box and grant or allow yourself to revolve around life.

Some people believe that the kind of life they live is due to the career they have chosen. While this can be true to them, those of a different view regarding this see life differently from a job.

What is there in life after a career? To be honest, True life is not a career but the example of life that Jesus came to live and show us as humans to follow, and as we live that life, we come into real life.

Knowledge of God, which we get when we read his word, plus obedience to what has been read and heard, equals a life that practically releases inner life to us as humans.

One of the major issues that teachers and other educational professionals are facing today is this. Let us face it. Anybody who has been in an education career ten years or more especially will tell you, almost consistently, that their view of practice and their role in it has changed dramatically over what it once was even a few short years ago.

Of course, some of this is just a shift in different attitudes as we age, but in my opinion, some of this also is deeply rooted in the number of challenges that we are faced with, with ever-increasing frequency. The more challenges you face determines how far you would go in life, so enjoy it. When circumstances change, you also change to cope with them.

Well, I hope you see where I am going here. Are you going through the "changes"? Somehow, years have passed since graduation, and life is not quite what you had imagined.

One of the significant consequences of this that I see every day in counseling is people in their early 30s to mid-50s who have a challenging time producing the fun and fulfillment in their work that not too long ago seemed natural and comfortable.

With all this said, I have some practical suggestions.

Evaluate Your Level of Control

Sometimes it is all too effortless to become fixated on events over which we have no power, capacity, or people who might never change their actions or attitude. But rather than focus on attributing blames to others or moving, the unmovable, resilient individuals set their sights on what they can control. To assess and evaluate your level of control over a situation, you can ask or challenge yourself, "What can I take responsibility for in this situation?" When you notice or look for opportunities to empower yourself and work towards a possible change, you are less likely to sense or feel stuck in difficult and challenging positions.

Practice Self-Care After a Loss

Often, life's transitions involve losses, such as a death, a big move, the loss of a job, or a relationship ending. Even positive shifts, like a convocation or a job change, can make you feel heartbroken. During these times of transition, do not push away any agony you might feel. Acknowledge the loss or disaster, and pay attention to what you have learned and gained from experience.

Seek support and camaraderie among colleagues, friends, and family, and consider speaking with a counselor or other mental health professional if you feel you need extra help during the transition.

Check Your Thought Patterns

In times of change, it is easy for your mind to cut corners. You might see everything in black and white, or you presume the worst will occur. But if you take the time to ponder and examine your thought patterns and assess how rational they are, you might find some space to nudge your thinking towards resilience. If you are not sure how to slow down your mind, practicing relaxation techniques, such as mindfulness or deep breathing, can help you feel more in control of your brain and how you evaluate a significant change transition.

You can also generate more conclusive positive reflective thoughts if you take the time to remember and remind yourself about the transitions and challenges you successfully navigated in the past. Make a list of ways you have been resilient in your life, and consider what peculiarity, traits, and actions might be able to see you through the current test or challenge. Focusing on your energy and strengths instead of your weaknesses will make you feel more empowered to meet what lies ahead.

Be in the Present

While it is essential to look to the past to find your

vigor, strengths, sometimes you can feel too pulled into the future in times of change. When you are apprehensive or worry about what the future will bring or what mistakes you might make, you forget to be present and observe what is happening around you. To bring yourself back to the now, get in tune with your body. Pay consideration to how it responds to stress, and set aside time every day to relax, take some deep breaths, and bring your focus back to the present.

Find Your Priorities

The most resilient individuals see change as an opportunity rather than a beast or monster to fear. Transitions in life avow you to consider where your priorities lie. How do you want to use your time on earth? What is essential to you? Where do you see yourself dissipating your time and energy? With a clear crystal sense of your goals and values, you will find your mind and body more resilient when changing stressors.

Above all, you prioritize your health in life's transitions meaning not being afraid to ask for help when you need it. Human beings are social creatures by essence and nature, so you were not built to withstand every sudden event in life without others' support. Talk to friends and families experiencing similar changes, or consider finding a support group in your community. Ask your doctor about prioritizing your health during the transition and not being afraid to talk to a counselor or other health professional about building resilience. You cannot avoid change, but you can live a life of stability. You can embrace transition and see tests or challenges as opportunities to thrive.

TIPS ON HOW TO CONQUER AND SUBDUE THE FEAR OF A NEW LIFE

The idea of starting over is both exciting and fearful. Exciting because you get to begin again, but with the knowledge and skills you already have in your arsenal. On the other hand, the fear part is usually because starting over is still full of uncertainties. If you are the anxious kind, then you probably feel the latter more.

Fear of the unknown is a natural body response when faced with something that feels uncertain, and it is entirely normal. However, succumbing to the fear of starting a new life can also result in you not living your best life. You absolutely would not want to miss those opportunities, and we are here to encourage you to take a leap of faith.

Here are tips on how to overcome the fear of starting a new life:

- **Look back at your motivation**. Each person has their respective reasons for why they want to begin a new life. Whether it is a job opportunity outside the country or something else, knowing the root of your new-life decision will determine what changes or improvements you want to see. Similarly, those experiences you want to change in your life will give you courage and push you to start over.
- **Envision the future you want**. The underlying motivation to your decision to start fresh should not only exist to jumpstart your decision. Instead, you should always have the outcome you want in your head. It will be easy to distract someone not working in the service of a dream. Set your achievable and time-bound goals in building that future you want, then always envision these results. Knowing the path to take is but a single step, but knowing where to go will make your walk into the new life clearer. That is less of the fears now.

- **Accept the fact that failures happen**. There is no point in lying to yourself and denying it anyway. Nor will we advise that "you will not fail" but "fear not because failures are not painful." They will happen, and they do hurt. But accepting that they exist and preparing yourself for the worst possible case scenario lessens the fears of starting over. Aside from this, you can devise ways to prevent it from happening.
- **There is no growth in comfort zones**. Creating a new life is not only exciting but even more challenging. It is like entering a decision-making game, but you are the main protagonist. This is what makes life exciting - the challenge of living. When you get comfortable, you become stagnant. You become used to your complacent and sedentary lifestyle. Life is thrilling when there are challenges. You get to know more of yourself when you are exposed outside your box.

Yes, it is a scary and uncertain decision. But taking it may be life-changing if you learn to calculate and assess the pros and cons of every scenario. Do not be afraid of starting new. You will do great, and we believe in you!

HOW TO PULL YOURSELF TOGETHER AFTER FAILING

Failure is painful and inevitable. Sooner or later, you will come to realize that you are not the best, even in your field of expertise. But will this reality get in the way of your path to success? If there is one truth, you must realize that the road to success is anything but smooth. There will always be bumps. There will always be slumps. It will hurt your ego, but then again, will a hurt ego stop you?

Take it from Oprah Winfrey. She said, "failure is another stepping stone to greatness." And she is entirely accurate. Failure is the best teacher, after all. Remember that being defeated or failing is not the end of your journey. It merely means you did not get it right the first time.

Getting back on track depends heavily on how you handle the failure. You can simply sit back, cry, and let it paralyze your being, or you can stand up and continue fighting. Everything is in your hands. But we are glad to give you a helping hand in your time of defeat. With that in mind, here are a few tips on how to pull yourself after failing:

- **Accept the truth.** There is no point in denying that you lost the battle. Accept the truth. It begins there. You failed now, but it is not the end of the world. Failing is okay, and failing today is not definitive of what will happen tomorrow. If so, then we would not have met Steve Jobs, Bill Gates, JK Rowling, Jack Ma, and a long list of failures turned into the world's most successful people.
- **Do not pin the blame on anyone.** The most common defense mechanism people do to cope with loss is looking for other people to blame. The truth of the matter is, the only one to blame is yourself. Take full responsibility for the failure. If you keep blaming others, then it is like having your success depends on them. Success and failure are in your hands.
- **Identify where you went wrong.** Whatever materialized in the past can no longer be redone and reversed. But we can always learn from the past. Get as much information from your failure. What were your

weaknesses, and what were your strengths? List them down and hone the areas where you think you lacked effort. Remember that it is "pulling yourself" from failure, which means that it is an active process. You do not remain in your broken state, but you press on toward the goal despite the brokenness. You do things that will improve yourself.

- **Toughen yourself from the setbacks.** As Rudy Francisco puts it, "muscle is created by repeatedly lifting things that have been designed to weigh us down." Every time you get back up from failing, remember that you become more challenging, healthier, and better. Soon enough, you will shrug off every failure you get and come backpacking a more potent punch.

Failure is a part of life. It adds to the thrill of living, and if we do not learn to step out of our comfort zones, then it is like we are not even living at all. Triumph at every success and learn from every failure, but do not ever stay where you are as of now. Always push to be at the top.

SECRETS OF SUCCESS FOR ADULTS

*A*s an adult, you are definitely in search of progress, right? So why not make it as simple as possible? Use these eight straightforward steps right now to put yourself on the path to achieving what you want in a short amount of time.

There are many frameworks for progress out there, but what works for you is not always what works for everyone else. Here is how you can apply the categories of passion, work, focus, push, ideas, improve, serve, persist, and balance as adults.

Passion

This area rarely seems to be a problem for adults. They have more trouble trying to limit or narrow down their passions than they do try to find one in the first place.

So as far as passion goes, select the one that stands out the most for you right now and thinks about what you could do to make it neat, impactful, and bump on the world.

This zeal will be one foundational piece of your fun dental mission - the path that will give you the ultimate excitement, pleasure, and satisfaction in life. You will possibly find that many of your great and impactful passions will fit together to formulate your essential mission entirely over time. And when that happens, you will be in an incredible place!

Work

However, you would like to consider it. It will take a lot of work to get to the climax of your life experience and involvement. Time, sweat, effort, money, and tears are all involved here.

The essential thing to remember as you are putting in vast amounts of effort, and being gifted, are likely on an emotional roller coaster for a good part of the time, is that every step of the way is getting you closer to where you want to be. Even if it does not look related to it, or if everyone around you is telling you that you are wasting your time, know that every learning experience makes you a more knowledgeable and more robust person who can handle the progress that comes at the top.

Focus

The things that you yen for in life will not necessarily drop into your lap - you will have to work for them - but you'll find that they will all come together much more quickly when you've determined your focus or focal point. You know for sure, or at minimum, mostly for sure, what you are aspiring for. (Not having a fixate focus is kind of like deciding to go on holiday but not knowing where. When you choose your destination, it makes getting there a whole lot easier.)

For adults, finding focus means doing one thing very well and figuring out how to use the many things you do well to make a difference in the lives of yourself and others. It is not about narrowing your focus down to such a point that it includes only one thing. It is about combining your many compass issues to create something new, exciting, and unexplored.

Push

This is one of the utmost trying parts of the process for gifted adults. Usually, the aims they have in life are not the traditional ones that most individuals shoot for. The things that bring them the most peace of mind are what may not be understood by many of the individuals closest to them. So, what do they do? This is where making connections with other skilled and gifted grownups are mandatory.

It is tough enough to progress at doing ordinary things, so you must set up your support systems in a big way when you are ready to move at an ultimate unconventional level. When you begin to feel down and out, when the work is becoming overwhelming, or when you feel like you are not even sure you are on the right track, getting in touch with your gifted friends can offer you the push you so definitely need that moment in time.

Ideas

Generating objectives and ideas is also something that usually comes relatively easy for gifted grownups. The challenge or test for them is to figure out which ones to use right now and which ones to place on the back burner for a while.

Keeping a journal or note is very helpful for this, as it will be having some tremendous let's-bang-around-some-great-ideas discussions with gifted friends. You can use or adapt some local or reachable experts in the fields you are working with, which will refine your reflections and insights. And suppose independent, do-it-now kind of idea creation is what you prefer. In that case, you can try setting up a filing cabinet with folders or compartments for each of your magnificent ideas, along with the supplies they need to put them into action.

Improve

This one more given for many gifted grownups. You can say it or have it built-in directly somehow. For them, the desire to reform and revamp is less like a potential option and more like a life-giving necessity.

Sometimes, for adults, the desire to improve is so strong that what to do or how to go about it in the best way becomes more of a challenge. Using the connections you have made with positive and uplifting people will help you figure out where the most important places are for you to progress from the position you are standing in right now. And recall, with the high learning curve that giftedness brings, your area of improvement might be different tomorrow, and next week, and next month. Just know that it is OK.

Serve

This is one extra area that's nearly part of adults' genetic makeup - the need to give something besides themselves. The undisclosed for them is to put their unique sets of passions together to create something that maximally serves others.

You can do amazing things; you have got bucket loads of ideas and passions; you are not afraid to keep on trying, and you want to help individuals with what you do. So now scrutinize what you would love to do, be and have if you had all the space, money, and resources you needed at your fingertips, and then take the first traces toward making that real. Putting the pieces together to adjust the world, not just in any way, but most beneficially and positively, is the goal now.

Persist

Isn't it surprising that one of the critical traits of giftedness is also one of the eight keys to success?

The biggest challenge for adults here is not that they are not persistent - they so often are to an incredible degree - but that they keep moving forward when they are feeling down and out when the world goes against them and when their unconventional concept is just beginning to emerge into the conceptualizations of the rest of the planet. -- So perhaps the ultimate success question for gifted adults is this: If 6-7 of these secrets to success are built into them, why are they not all incredibly successful?

The most significant answer lies in Progress Point 4 - Push. At only 3-5% of the general population, grown-ups are so physically scattered in their cities, communities, and countries that they have trouble finding one another. And without other people who understand their intensities and what some may call insanities, it is hard to keep moving forward.

If you are a grown-up, be on the lookout for others like you anywhere and everywhere you go. And when you find them, hang onto them, especially the positive, motivating ones, because their presence around you may just be the final piece you need to complete the puzzle of your essential life mission and find ultimate progress.

Balance

Sometimes, you get caught up in chasing your dreams and passion, and it is not wrong. However, challenges arise when you fail to look over your personal life because you are too preoccupied with being the best in your field.

Too much work, no matter how noble the principle behind it, has negative repercussions. That is why a maintained life and work balance is essential. There must be time for work, but they're also must be allotted time for personal matters. Here are tips you can use to maintain your balance:

- **Assess your productivity schedule.** The first step starts from within. Know who you are. Are you a late-night owl or an early bird? By understanding the most productive period, you can assign the problematic tasks on that time frame and leave the relatively easy ones on the less productive hours. This way, your workload may be distributed according to your strengths and weaknesses.

- **Set a work period and strictly follow it**. It would be counter-intuitive to work office duties at night, so you are left with no other choice but to work during the day. By setting your mind to work on your 9-5 shift, you will be able to condition your body to be productive when your productivity needs it! This means more work was done during the day, with no overtime, and you can spend time with your family at home.
- **Learn to unplug when needed.** Work can be very stressful. Taking a breather is never wrong. If your work becomes too toxic and stressful, then take a step back and relax for a while. Grinding your head too much at work will diminish your enthusiasm and energy to continue. Unplugging from it for a while will not only be good for your mental and physical health, even more so, it will give you the positive vibe you need to get back to work after.

- **Be sure your health is at its best.** One common thing that lets you go off when one is swamped with work is exercising. Yes, your dues and deadlines are essential, but so is your health. When you postpone your evening jogs or weekend gyms, you only make room for stress to build in without releasing the tension. This will affect your life-work balance because there is no longer "life" flowing inside you. Take care of your health.
- **Make time for what matters most.** This tip goes both ways. Too much personal time leaves no room for work. On the other hand, too much work will burn you out. The information is about making time, not finding the time. Try to assess yourself. When you see an imbalance in your life schedule, make time for what matters most. Be it family, yourself, your friends, or even work if needed.

I remember an inspirational story that goes with our work-life balance topic.

The father was swamped with work and always went home late. He no longer had attention from his family. He then noticed his son continually asking for money from him. This system went on for some time. When the son collected enough, he gave it all back to his father and said: "Dad, this is equal to your salary. Can mom and I have your time for a month?" This broke him into tears and made him change his ways.

Work-life balance is essential. Check yourself. Maybe you are leaving something important behind.

PLEASE LEAVE A 1-CLICK REVIEW!

I hope you enjoyed reading this book!

If you haven't done so yet, I would be incredibly thankful if you could take 60 seconds to write a brief review on the platform of purchase, even if it's just a few sentences!

Your feedback will be a huge help in helping other readers benefit from the information in the book.

You can also contact us by sending an email to tcecpublishing@outlook.com

Like us on https://www.facebook.com/tcecpublishing/

Join our Facebook page : https://www.facebook.com/groups/800312427190446 to stay updated on our next releases!

See you there!

https://tcecpublishing.com/tcsf-free-ebook

CONCLUSION

Summing up, these are some of the ways you could take more responsibility in life. Taking all these steps mentioned in this book means that you are a mature adult. You do not let life go astray but stay healthy through the hard times without getting devastated and ruining yourself. Look out for the silver lining behind every cloud and be joyfully happy.

OTHER BOOKS YOU'LL LOVE!

1. Healthy Habits for Kids: Positive Parenting Tips for Fun Kids Exercises, Healthy Snacks and Improved Kids Nutrition
2. Mini Habits for Happy Kids: Proven Parenting Tips for Positive Discipline and Improving Kids' Behavior
3. Financial Tips to Help Kids: Proven Methods for Teaching Kids Money Management and Financial Responsibility
4. Life Strategies for Teenagers: Positive Parenting Tips and Understanding Teens for Better Communication and a Happy Family
5. 101 Tips for Child Development: Proven Methods for Raising Children and Improving Kids Behavior with Whole Brain Training

6. 101 Tips For Helping With Your Child's Learning: Proven Strategies for Accelerated Learning and Raising Smart Children Using Positive Parenting Skills
7. Parenting Teen Boys in Today's Challenging World: Proven Methods for Improving Teenagers Behaviour with Whole Brain Training
8. Parenting Teen Girls in Today's Challenging World: Proven Methods for Improving Teenagers Behaviour with Whole Brain Training
9. The Fear of The Lord: How God's Honour Guarantees Your Peace
10. Tips for #CollegeLife: Powerful College Advice for Excelling as a College Freshman
11. The Motivated Young Adult's Guide to Career Success and Adulthood: Proven Tips for Becoming a Mature Adult, Starting a Rewarding Career, and Finding Life Balance
12. Career Success Formula Proven Career Development Advice And Finding Rewarding Employment For Young Adults And College Graduates
13. Developing Yourself as a Teenager
14. Guide for Boarding School Life

REFERENCES

[1] https://www.selfgrowth.com/articles/Are_We_Adults.html

[2] https://www.dailyschoolnews.com.ng/score-high-in-post-utme/

[3] https://www.philosophytalk.org/shows/what-adult

[4] https://www.philosophytalk.org/blog/what-adult

[5] https://storybuilder.jumpstart.ge/en/sweet-voiced-cocodrile

[6] https://www.officialcharts.com/chart-news/looking-back-at-amy-winehouses-back-to-black-ten-10-years-on__15545/

[7] https://www.forbes.com/sites/marcusnoel/2018/06/25/magnate-ceo-rustin-keller-is-transporting-human-wellness-values-to-gen-z/

[8] https://fashionista.com/2019/04/natural-beauty-myths-claims-facts-debunked

[9] https://teacher-blogdeaula.blogspot.com/2011_04_27_archive.html

[10] https://www.gilmorecommunication.com/results-level-2-combinations/

[11] https://esmemes.com/i/jaxkie-ajaxkkkie-as-you-get-older-you-start-to-see-bf65d72b99054d9b97acad9c2e1fa530

[12] https://www.webmd.com/mental-health/depersonalization-disorder-mental-health

[13] https://www.mentalhelp.net/blogs/self-responsibility-self-accountability-qualifies-you-as-an-adult/

[14] https://www.newportfire.net/2020/06/16/four-things-that-can-help-you-advance-in-your-career/

[15] https://laborworks.com/tips-to-prepare-for-a-new-job-or-career/

[16] https://www.forbes.com/sites/francesbridges/2019/03/29/5-ways-to-be-a-more-positive-person/

[17] https://www.geico.com/information/life-stages/on-your-own/financial-responsibility-tips/

[18] https://www.stevepavlina.com/blog/2005/01/what-is-your-career/

[19] https://www.dubaicareerguide.com/uae-career-tips/what-exactly-is-your-career.htm

[20] https://crazzyjob.blogspot.com/

[21] https://campbell-north.com/blog/05-june-2018/graduate-advice-%E2%80%93-how-get-job-you-actually-want

[22] https://www.youtern.com/thesavvyintern/index.php/2013/09/15/in-3-steps-make-your-career-ah-ha-moment-happen/

[23] https://govalor.com/story/leading-well-in-tough-times/

[24] https://www.pickthebrain.com/11-important-things-know/

[25] https://perfectpracticeweb.com/going-through-the-changes/

[26] https://31baa9204011a4b7373d-4b45c627b478904b4d98bc32b4be9291.ssl.cf2.rackcdn.com/uploaded/c/0e10020884_1585084882_counseling-corner-psychology-of-copng-with-change-3-20.pdf

[27] https://www.erikamohssen-beyk.com/better-mind/6-effective-ways-to-cope-with-big-changes/

[28] https://kuulpeeps.com/2019/05/24/uew-here-are-tips-on-how-to-overcome-the-exam-fear/kuulife

[29] https://www.happierhuman.com/use-affirmations/

[30] https://medium.com/synapse/the-first-five-years-lessons-learned-from-five-years-of-teaching-cad6401ea7d7

[31] https://www.marcandangel.com/2014/02/16/15-things-you-must-give-up-to-be-happy-again/

[32] https://blogs.findlaw.com/in_house/2018/11/businesswomen-who-failed-then-won.html

[33] http://blog.learnleo.com/passing-the-bar/

[34] https://personalitybuzz.com/are-you-an-early-bird-or-a-night-owl/

[35] https://www.dumblittleman.com/how-to-overcome-failure/

[36] https://businessbrokendown.com/2016/01/18/how-to-motivate-yourself-in-times-of-failure/

[37] https://www.success.com/13-inspiring-quotes-about-failure/

[38] https://build.wanderingaimfully.com/blog/fear-of-starting-something-new

[39] https://www.powerofpositivity.com/therapists-explain-6-ways-to-overcome-the-fear-of-starting-again/

[40] https://curlsandcocoa.com/how-to-start-a-new-life/

[41] https://www.lifecoach-directory.org.uk/blog/2017/08/07/5-things-when-out-of-love-with-job

[42] https://projecteve.com/12-signs-that-youve-fallen-out-of-love-with-career/

[43] https://www.businessnewsdaily.com/5244-improve-work-life-balance-today.html

[44] https://www.roche.com/careers/our-locations/asia/india/service/folder/20_tips_for_maintain.htm

[45]   https://www.forbes.com/sites/deborahlee/2014/10/20/6-tips-for-better-work-life-balance/#3e762f0229ff

[46]   https://www.skillsyouneed.com/ps/work-life-balance.html

www.ingramcontent.com/pod-product-compliance
Lightning Source LLC
Chambersburg PA
CBHW071622080526
44588CB00010B/1228